What People Are Saying

Harness Your ZEBRA *will help many emerging artists who have not had the guidance they need. Adria Firestone is filling a gap, and her vast stage experience will inspire her readers. Between college and the professional stage are pitfalls, challenges, dreams and disappointments. Sometimes these overwhelm young performers. Adria Firestone, a talented performer who has seen it all, provides guidance, encouragement and practical tools which help any young artist face the real world. This book is a "must read" for serious young performers.*

~ Ian D. Campbell, General Director and Artistic Director, San Diego Opera

Harness Your ZEBRA *is loaded with exercises to support the career quest of any performer. In fact, many of us could utilize this book for our daily lives. I applaud Adria for finally addressing the "nitty-gritty" of what singers and performers should address before, during and after they commit to their professional careers. Bravo! Well done and impeccably organized!*

~ Donna Connolly, Co-Chair Music, Dance & Theater, & Vocal Coordinator
New Jersey City University

I'm happy to see a book that finally explains the how of professional performance and show business. It is a business, and although we learn about the art in school, nobody tells us anything about how to get a job keep it and land the next one. The ZEBRA method addresses the people, temperaments, functions and pitfalls of working professionally. Adria is one professional who really knows her stuff, I know – I've worked with her.

~ Robin L. Gray, Actors Equity Stage Manager, 30+ years

This book is so user friendly and informative. From the moment you open it you feel like you've stepped into a performance workshop. This book is a must for anyone who wants to improve their craft.

~ Grace Valdes, Performer

This book is not only reader friendly and informative, but arguably should be considered required reading for all performing artists. The anecdotes are terrific. You may also quote me when I say that it should be in the library of every school in the country with a music and performing arts department!

~ Michael Hirsch, Actor /Director/Composer

What dawned on me is that there is a great kindness about this book. I have never seen/felt it before in a text or how-to book. There is kindness from the author to the reader, from the reader to himself; from the reader to others. . . The book itself feels as if it is a Zen space. I prefer to read paper books, so I absolutely cannot wait to have one in my hot little hands!

~ Carol Hannan, Counselor, Educator, 35 years Los Angeles Public School System

ZEBRA *puts into words exactly what helped me become a better performer when I was in Adria's studio! She knows how to turn vision into visceral reality and can make a clumsy dodo bird soar like a proud eagle. Reading this will help take you to the next level and become the performer you want to be. This book is a must-read for anyone even thinking about stepping foot on stage, whether it's community theatre or the Great White Way.*

~ Lauren Bock Mullins, MM in performance

Ride that ZEBRA! Adria Firestone does an amazing job of communicating to performers how to shed the layers of fear and equip us with tools to grab audiences and take them along for the ride. I've certainly learned a lot from this truly powerful woman's words; thank goodness she's written them down for us all to own and remind us that we can push through our chains and pull the audience in.

~Ema Mitrovic, Mezzo-Soprano

As a playwright, this book gave me a new appreciation of how to schedule and utilize my time better. I am getting more done in less time. Adria Firestone and ZEBRA gave me the tools to do it.

~ Vincent D'Onofrio, playwright, author of *Defense of Doubt & Gang Priest*

Harness Your ZEBRA, *asks, addresses and answers the questions that can take an artist who was once sitting in a prison cell with the door wide open, to a stage; performing for thousands of people with ease. I am living proof that when the content of this book is applied, the artist WILL see results. These tools work to build your dream. If you aspire to be an artist, drink in this wisdom.*

~Julianne Park, MM, opera singer, music teacher, Project leader at Sing for Hope NYC

In working with Adria Firestone I attained new performance heights. She helped me 'unclutter' my performing while encouraging the most creative and expressive energy to flow. **Harness Your ZEBRA** *is a succinct and easy to follow manual to help in the pursuit of executing powerful performance art. I will recommend it to my students who wish to pursuit performance careers.*

~ Denise R. Mitchell, Certified Music Teacher, Graduate Student Opera Performance

After an extensive international career as an opera singer, Adria Firestone has used her wealth of skills to perform in musicals, cabarets, horror films, and handle a voiceover gig for Family Guy. Whether working as a performer or a personal coach, she is a sharp-witted woman who can spot many opportunities faster than most.

I first witnessed Adria's social dexterity in Egypt, as she jokingly took over negotiating the price (in camels) for a date with one of her colleagues in the cast of Show Boat. Since then, Adria has continued to demonstrate an intense curiosity about the world as it was, as it is, and as it continues to emerge around her. In addition to sharing her critical knowledge of homeopathy and natural supplements, Adria's self-help manual for artists – **Harness Your ZEBRA** *– offers a no-nonsense guide for aspiring musicians that will quickly separate the wannabes from the professionals.*

Harness Your ZEBRA *explains, in easily understandable language, how to deal with stress, stage fright, and criticism while having a suitcase packed and ready to handle unexpected challenges. Not only does it teach artists how to treat their bodies, their work, and their future as a business, it explains how to avoid clumsy, costly ego-driven mistakes (on the Internet as well as in real life).*

In an electronically-connected world, performers whose professional lives can keep them on the road for months at a time can learn a lot from Adria Firestone about how to keep their integrity and sanity intact while sharpening their entrepreneurial instincts, building their brand, strengthening their performance skills and deepening their artistic impact.

~George Heymont, San Francisco-based arts critic and contributor to *The Huffington Post*

Harness Your ZEBRA

Career Design & Power Performance for the Emerging Performing Artist

Adria Firestone

STONEFIRE PRESS

© 2012 Adria Firestone. All rights reserved. No part of this book may be reproduced or transmitted in any form by any means, electronic, mechanical, photocopying, recording, or otherwise, without the prior written permission of the publisher.

Published by StoneFire Press, a division of Adria Firestone International, LLC.

Find us on the web at www.AdriaFirestone.com
To report errors, please send a note to errata@adriafirestone.com

"I Whistle a Happy Tune" by Richard Rodgers and Oscar Hammerstein II
Copyright © 1951 by Richard Rodgers and Oscar Hammerstein II
Copyright renewed. International copyright secured. All rights reserved.
Used by permission of Williamson Music, a division of Rodgers & Hammerstein:
An Imagem Company

Notice of liability
Information in this book is distributed as an "as is" basis, without warranty. While every precaution has been taken in the preparation of the book, neither the author nor StoneFire Press nor Adria Firestone International, LLC shall have any liability to any person or entity with respect to any loss or damage caused or alleged to be caused directly or indirectly by the instructions contained in this book or by the computer software, hardware, herbal or medical products described in it.

ISBN 13: 978-0-9835537-3-1

*To Lee A. Olsen whose vision, confidence
in me, and unwavering support, nurtured me as an artist and a person.
To Charles Kingsford, composer and mentor who fostered
continuous learning.*

Table of Contents

Foreword		11
Introduction	**Your Performance Dreams**	13
PART ONE	**PREPARE FOR THE ZEBRA METHOD**	
Chapter 1	**The ZEBRA Method: What's In It for You?**	17
	Minimize fear maximize expression	17
	How do we learn to learn?	17
	Excellence takes time	18
	What is the ZEBRA method?	18
	Benefits you will receive	18
	The magic of mastery	19
	Are you self-motivated?	19
	Summary	21
	Exercises	22
Chapter 2	**What is This Thing Called Fear?**	33
	What is performance anxiety?	33
	When does the fear begin?	33
	Parents and peers	34
	Unconscious imitation	34
	Change your present	35
	Comparison	35
	Personal experience	36
	Get an education but perform continuously	36
	Experiment with different styles	36
	In the middle of success	37
	Is there a magic solution?	37
	Summary	38
	Exercises	39
Chapter 3	**Performer – Know Thyself**	47
	Getting to know you	47
	Hardcore questions	48
	Take the evaluations to heart	48
	Make the average superior	49
	Plan B	49
	Why do you perform?	50
	The antenna of the race	50
	The magic of sharing	51
	What are you afraid of?	51
	Fail better	52
	Personal experience	52
	Summary	54
	Exercises	55

Chapter 4	**Do Drugs – You'll Feel Much Better, or Not**	**69**
	Aromatherapy	69
	Aromatherapy – the negative kind	70
	Homeopathic remedies	70
	Alcohol	71
	Herbal remedies	71
	Other helpful options	72
	Food as medicine	72
	Prescription options	72
	Is it illegal? Dangerous?	73
	Performance enhancers and enablers	73
	The rare 1%	75
	A club for shy souls	75
	The debate goes on	75
	Summary	76
	Exercises	77
Chapter 5	**The People in the Dark**	**81**
	Make friends with the enemy	81
	Change your focus	81
	Create a bubble	82
	The magic of the present	82
	Sharing vs. showing off	83
	Personal experience	84
	Use the nervous energy	84
	If you make a mistake	85
	After the performance	85
	How to criticize constructively	86
	After performance questions	87
	To film or not to film	87
	Summary	89
	Exercises	90
Chapter 6	**Your Not-So-Secret Weapon**	**103**
	The audiovisual world	103
	The internet	104
	Email and communication	104
	You are your own press agent	105
	Your website	105
	Answers your website must provide	106
	Research saves you time and money	106
	Research your future employers	107
	Social media, pros and cons	107
	Summary	109
	Exercises	110

PART TWO — THE ZEBRA METHOD

Chapter 7 — Z is for Your Zen Studio — 117
- The ZEBRA structure — 117
- The mental space — 118
- The physical space — 119
- Budget time and energy — 119
- Learn the skill first — 119
- Time off — 120
- What am I aiming for? — 120
- Learn how to learn — 120
- Before the performance — 120
- Personal experience — 121
- Review the past — 121
- The performance — 121
- The lists — 122
- Summary — 123
- Exercises — 124

Chapter 8 — E is for Eliminate Your Negative Self-talk — 133
- Awareness is the first step — 133
- Accentuate the positive — 133
- Write a new script — 134
- Write out the negative characters — 135
- Face your fears — 135
- Stay present — 136
- Common distortions — 136
- The attitude of gratitude — 137
- Take the time you need — 137
- Summary — 139
- Exercises — 140

Chapter 9 — B is for Be Prepared — 165
- Work backwards — 165
- Rehearse deliberately — 165
- Learn it first — 166
- Learn from the best — 166
- Learn it by heart — 166
- Normal preparation — 167
- Emergency preparation — 167
- Personal experience — 168
- How the pros do it — 168
- Can you be too prepared? — 169
- Summary — 170
- Exercises — 171

Chapter 10	**R is for Relaxation & Ritual**	**179**
	What is relaxation?	179
	Physical relaxation	180
	Mental relaxation	180
	Personal experience	181
	Out of our headspace	181
	What is best for you?	182
	The Cycle of Nine	182
	Benefits	182
	What is ritual?	184
	Plan ahead but be flexible	184
	Summary	185
	Exercises	186
Chapter 11	**A is for 'Act as if'**	**189**
	Can you whistle?	189
	Body language	189
	Put your head on your shoulders	190
	What is your body saying?	190
	Positive self-deception	192
	Don't forget to breathe	192
	Make-believe	193
	Personal experience	193
	Wrap up	194
	Summary	195
	Exercises	196
	Notes	**203**
	Bibliography	**205**
	Acknowledgements	**207**
	About the Author	**209**

Foreword

We live in a world where we feel less and less in control. Singers and performers are notorious control freaks, which is the very trait that can ultimately undermine their success. We live in a world of visibility, instant fame, hyperbole, materialism and more. We often forget that we have choices. As a singer, I know that it is easy to forget that I am not my voice. When one's talent is mostly on the inside it is easy to lapse into this way of thinking: perhaps that is why we are called sensitive or temperamental.

Adria Firestone outlines clear, practical ways how to make choices; choices from everything from one's mind-set to external influences. From someone who has been through it all and continues to find new ways to create, Adria gives us great tools for creative performing artists to get a sense of self and place in our ever busy and changing world and industry. She has her finger on the pulse of the hurdles performing artists always face.

Harness your ZEBRA is a perfect title not just from the standpoint of the anagram but also the metaphor of a zebra as an artist - a shy creature, prey for large cats, hyenas and dogs (coincidentally, all monikers we often assign to people in the business). A zebra can at times blend in and at other times stand out with its unique markings which are unlike those of any other zebra. They can be solitary and they can herd.

I sure do wish this book had been around when I was a young singer. It might have saved me endless grief, counseling and self-doubt and helped me to control the things I could.

Susanne Mentzer
Opera Singer, Professor of Voice
Blogger for *The Huffington Post*

Your Performance Dreams

This book is a how-to manual to turn your performance dreams into professional, sustainable reality. We the artists, the actors, singers, musicians, dancers and backstage wizards spend all we make on refining our skills. We aim for mastery of our chosen passion, but what about reality, clarity and action? Where do we learn how to get on a realistic career track? Right here in this book.

We learn skills and are not taught what to do with these skills in the real world. We do not know how to ground ourselves in a solid framework of practical study, planning, assessment, business and marketing. The methods taught in this volume lessen anxiety, encourage growth and allow us to keep the very thing a lack of focus causes us to lose - the love of our craft that got us started in the first place.

Are you tired of leaving your best performance in the studio? Would you like to achieve your goals with less anxiety? In this book, you will answer penetrating questions for assessment of your talent and ability. You will learn to stop rehearsing your mistakes. Have you done the work and it doesn't show? You will learn how to transform your fear into focus.

Enter ZEBRA

What on earth do zebras have to do with performance? **ZEBRA is a method that allows a performer to progress from amateur to professional in clear, practical and measurable steps.** It is "Zen-like" in its serene, methodical approach to learning, auditioning and performing.

You will learn:
- To **rehearse calmly, anytime and anywhere** in your mental "Zen studio."
- To **use less energy and achieve more in less time**.
- A **method of working that is uniquely your own,** balanced by downtime.
- To **raise your level of performance** to consistent professionalism.

This is not a book about the *theory* of performance. From age ten, I was on stage: I have lived and breathed theater my entire life. I learned from the best in our business. I earned my living making music all over the world. I know what works and what does not. My way is not the only way, but it is a great starting point to achieve your performance dreams.

On this journey to professional artistry, you will gather tools that will benefit not only your craft, but your life. Behind the curtain, we are all colleagues no matter what branch of the arts is our passion. Without each other, there is no light and we can't shine.

I salute you all and wish you a world of success,

Adria Firestone
Jersey City, NJ

PART ONE

Prepare for the ZEBRA Method

*Every day we choose what script we will write for ourselves,
how we will play our part, what wardrobe we will wear,
and what emotions we will allow ourselves to feel or to repress.
I don't know whether I chose acting or acting chose me in this life.
Either way, I am the writer, producer, wardrobe mistress, star,
and director of my own play every day that I live.*
— Shirley MacLaine, *I'm Over All That*

Chapter One

The ZEBRA Method: What's In It for You?

If you want to distance yourself from the masses and enjoy a unique lifestyle, understand this – your habits will determine your future.
— *Canfield, Hanson, Hewitt,* The Power of Focus

Do you know what it takes to be a working professional? When you stand up to perform, do your knees turn to jelly? Do you know how to realistically assess your ability? Do you know what your goal is and do you have a plan to get there?

Here is a diagnostic question: in spite of all the nerves and all the sacrifice, are you in love with the stage? Does the thought of being an actor, singer, dancer, or instrumentalist make your eyes glow? Does it make your heart beat faster?

If any of these questions strike a receptive chord in you - alas! You have been bitten and there is no known cure. I think Ella Fitzgerald said it best, *"The only thing better than singing is more singing."* Replace 'singing' with your artistic passion and the diagnosis remains the same.

I have been on your journey. I ran away to life upon the wicked stage because nothing I could imagine was more beautiful than the theater. For over thirty years it was my home and my refuge. The stage was my safe space. It is where I grew up along with the characters I created. It was also the place where I learned a great deal about myself.

Minimize fear maximize expression
I have been teaching at New Jersey City University for over seven years. In the past twenty years, I have given innumerable international master classes, seminars and workshops. From San Diego to Singapore, Abu Dhabi to Kalamazoo, no matter where I go, it is always the same. Fear gets in the way of our artistic expression.

Each time I speak about stage fright, performance or career development with students, their response is: "So, where's the book?" ZEBRA is that book. The ZEBRA method offers more artistic freedom, a more direct path to powerful performance and a practical way to design a professional career.

There are wonderful books out there. Some of my favorites are listed on my website. A reviewer from Denmark said of one of the books: "I needed a dictionary to understand this book, but it was worth it." That remark inspired me to get clear, simple, and very direct. The ZEBRA method clarifies the path between talented amateur and professional. No dictionary needed!

How do we learn how to learn?
Universities and schools teach us all the beautiful literature, plays, songs, and concertos. They teach us how to bow and how to breathe. But often, we are not taught how to learn in an organized way so we can recreate what we've learned again and again.

Instead of blaming ourselves for mistakes, we need to analyze what went wrong. We need to take it apart and put it back together. We need to practice slowly and methodically until the mistake is permanently eradicated. Does that sound like a long procedure? It's not instantaneous; I'll give you that.

This method of understanding what went wrong and correcting it eliminates fear. *Repeating what is correct imprints the confidence the same mistake won't happen again.* A music coach I know can't stand it when students say: "Oh darn, I *always* make that mistake." His question to me was: "If they *always* make that mistake, why haven't they corrected it?" Why indeed?

Excellence takes time

Very few things of quality happen instantaneously. When I first began piano lessons, I wanted to sit down and immediately play the *Moonlight Sonata*. It didn't happen. I did not have the patience or the follow-through to practice in a way that would make me an accomplished pianist. However, I had enough passion and commitment to practice the skills that made me a fine singer and actress. Again, it didn't happen overnight.

The ZEBRA method asks you to give yourself all the time you need to polish the technical aspects of any piece you are learning. Only then, can you go to the next level and imbue every moment with your unique imprint. Then you can color it with your artistry and your passion.

When you get in the habit of working this way you may suddenly leap ahead of where you were two days ago. But no matter how large the leap, excellence is best played as a game of one on one – you with yourself. Ask yourself: Can I top what I did five months ago? Or five minutes ago? If that desire and spark leaves, it is time to reconsider what you are doing.

What is the ZEBRA method?

Are you ready to experience a practical way to achieve your performance goals and harness mental toughness? The ZEBRA method increases relaxation and lowers anxiety. My method will help you:

- Z - Create a mental **"Zen" studio** where you visualize and train for excellence.
- E - **Eliminate the negative script** running in your head.
- B - **Be prepared**; learn the art and science of organized preparation.
- R - Discover which **relaxation methods** work for you.
- A - "**Act as if**," harness mental discipline and toughness**.**

Benefits you will receive

Your internal Zen studio (think of quiet focus, not religion) is a mental space that allows you to be mindful of your present level of expertise. It is the place to visualize the steps needed for your success. It allows you to work with focus and compassion on self-development. This is the place where you unfold the ZEBRA method.

You will discover a clear, concise method of study that calms nerves, relieves anxiety and makes your positive results repeatable. In other words, you won't have to wait for inspiration to hit you to be able to play Chopin's *Polonaise* well. You will know where the pitfalls are because you have methodically worked through the problem spots, not only physically, but mentally.

The ability to perform well with a consistent level of excellence is what separates the amateurs from the professionals. This method supplies the tools for you to create habits that lead to success. A standard of excellence will become habit. Occasionally, if you are fortunate, you will have extraordinary moments of inspiration that will carry both you and your audience away. Other times you may fall slightly below your normal standard. It is when you begin preparing and producing at a consistent level that you pass from the level of an amateur to possibly earning a living at what you love.

You notice I said *possibly*. There are no guarantees in this business. There are no guarantees in life. No matter how talented you are, no matter your level of excellence, you may not have Glinda, the good witch of the North, on your shoulder. You may have to earn your living another way. That is reality.

The magic of mastery
Effortless mastery is irresistible. But how do we achieve that mastery? Consistency is part of mastery. Consistency allows you to give fine performances, time after time. Control is also an element of mastery. You need to be able to control the way you think and act in a stressful situation. Control, thought of in another way, is mental toughness. It doesn't matter whether you're shy or bold, introverted or extroverted. No matter how shy you are, you can learn mental toughness. It is also Zen mindfulness.

The reward of sticking to, and mastering, a skill gives such a sense of personal satisfaction that it heightens your pleasure in performance. Finally, the pleasure begins to overwhelm and outweigh the anxiety. There is nothing more exhilarating for an artist to experience her own mastery. An audience thrills to observe a master at work. To have seen Carla Fracci, the exquisite Italian ballerina, was to observe poetry in motion. Her smile was not frozen in a rehearsal mirror. It reflected the real joy she felt as she danced.

Are you self-motivated?

> *Successful people don't drift to the top. It takes focused action,*
> *personal discipline and lots of energy every day to make things happen.*
> — Canfield, Hansen, Hewitt, *The Power of Focus*

No matter how many systems or methods you use, there are keys that make all of them work. Two of them are your own passion and determination to succeed. You need to be self-motivated and self-directed. You need a strong ability to visualize and commit to the steps necessary to realize your own success. You need to be realistic but positive when you assess your performance. When problems inevitably arise, you must learn to view them as challenges. You need to be able to concentrate and focus intensely.

All you can control is the present. You can learn from your past mistakes. Release the past and keep only the lessons. The future is not in your control: you're not there yet. All you have is this moment to hone and refine your present skills. *You need to be able to control your mental attitude and harness your energy, no matter how you're feeling.* These qualities are an essential part of mental toughness and mindfulness.

Most of the time as a professional, you will not perform at your optimum level. There are so many factors in the way. You may be ill, have allergies, traveled for days or be in a difficult performance situation. However, you will be able to control a great deal with your technique and your mental toughness, because you have trained yourself well.

That difference in attitude, in control, is what sets apart the handful of successful people from the thousands who fall by the wayside. The challenge is to be able to learn your way around and master your most important instrument: you. When you control your mind, you can control the steps you take to reach your goals and to a great extent, your level of performance.

There is a hidden gift in this book. We are talking about performance skills here, right? Do you realize almost everything relates to your life as well? Your attitude and your preparation set you up for success or failure. I offer the challenge. Do you accept it?

Chapter One: Summary

To **minimize fear and maximize expression**, instead of blaming ourselves for our mistakes, we need to:
- **Analyze** what went wrong.
- **Take it apart.**
- **Put it back together.**
- **Practice slowly and methodically** – until the mistake is *permanently* gone.

Your internal Zen studio is a mental space (not a religious concept) that allows you to be mindful of your present level of expertise and work with focus and compassion on self-development. This is the place where you unfold the ZEBRA method and train the habit of excellence.

Excellence takes time. Very few things of quality happen instantaneously.

Repeating what is correct imprints the confidence that the same mistake won't happen again.

The ZEBRA method asks you to **give yourself the time you need to polish the technical aspects of any piece you are learning.** Only then can you give artistry free reign.

The ZEBRA method:
- Z – Create an **internal Zen studio**.
- E – **Eliminate your negative script**.
- B – **Be prepared**.
- R – Find your **relaxation** methods.
- A – **Act 'as if'**

The ability to perform with **a consistent level of excellence is what separates the amateur from the professional.**

Consistency is part of mastery. Consistency allows you to give fine performances time after time, no matter the stress you're under.

Mental toughness and control is what sets apart the handful of successful people from the thousands who fall by the wayside.

You need to **be self-motivated and self-directed, with a strong ability to visualize** and commit to the steps necessary to realize your own success.

Successful people don't drift to the top!

Your attitude and your preparation set you up for success or failure.

Chapter One: Exercises

The exercises, charts and questions that follow each chapter offer different tools for learning about yourself and your craft. The ZEBRA method will help you define the reality of your potential and clarify what steps you need to take for your personal and professional success.

Organization and self-discovery will make your job a lot easier. Self-discovery is an ongoing process. In this process you will find out what your values are and if you live your life according to those values, you will uncover your needs. If you don't find out what those needs are, they will control you, hidden in your unconscious, but they will control you. Opt in at www.afiartists.com and give yourself the gift of the Needless Program from Coach Inc. Extraordinary stuff.

Now let us continue the most fascinating journey you will ever take not only as an artist, but as a human, the journey to yourself.

Your learning style

One of the most important things for you to find out is what is your dominant learning style, as well as what is your particular combination of learning styles. 60% of people are multimodal or have several learning styles. Knowing what works for you will make your learning process easier. Learning styles are usually divided into three groups:

- **Visual learners**: visual learners like to see what they're learning. They may take lots of detailed notes and close their eyes to visualize or remember something. They benefit from illustrations and presentations that use color and charts. They're attracted to written or spoken language that is rich in imagery. They like their surroundings to be neutral, so as not to distract them from their work.

- **Auditory learners**: auditory learners sometimes acquire knowledge by reading aloud. They may hum or talk to themselves when they get bored. (I even talk to myself when I'm not bored. ;-) They're very quick to learn music or lines or dialogue if they record it and then listen to it.

- **Kinesthetic learners**: kinesthetic learners need to take many breaks. They get physically restless if they have to sit still in one place for too long. They can remember what was done but they may forget what was said. They like to experience performance, rather than just sitting back and listening or watching. They like tasks where they can become physically involved. They use their hands and gestures to express themselves.

Links to learning styles

I found these links very helpful for tests you can take online that help you determine your learning style or your combination of learning styles. Take two or three of them and see if there's any difference between them.

- http://literacyworks.org/mi/intro/index.html
- http://people.usd.edu/~bwjames/tut/learning-stylest.html

Let me know what other tests you find and the ones that are most helpful to you.

Why do you perform?
I will ask you this question again in this book. My only requirement is that each time you write an answer to the question, it must be different from the answer you gave before. In this section, I want you to write as fast as you can without much thought.

Why do you perform? What does performing give you that nothing else does?

The one page business plan
Most people don't think of art and performance as a business. I assure you it is. Your desired career, no matter what it is, needs to be run with efficiency and direction. *If you don't know where you're going, you'll never get anywhere.* You must also be honest about your starting point. You can't get *there* from *here*, unless you know where *here* is.

Before you fill in the business plan, answer these questions:

What will my career in the arts look like?

In what ways will it fulfill me? What is the purpose of my career?

Will my vocation benefit the world in any way?

How will I measure my success?

What qualities will make my career successful?

What strategies or steps do I need to take to attain my vision?

Make copies of the blank business plan and start writing now. Work backwards from your vision.

SAMPLE BUSINESS PLAN FOR Violet Valery

Vision — What am I building?
- Within 5 years to have a thriving international career as a soloist.
- Have a balanced, quality, family life and a net worth of at least $500,000.00.

Mission — What is the purpose of my business?
- Enable all women in the USA through my music & my foundation to get a HS education & job training.
- Design better food distribution with other organizations. Not one child goes hungry or uneducated. USA first, then the world!

Objectives — What will I measure?
- Book 20 additional concerts @ min $5,000. net each
- Develop my marketing skills & barter for publicist
- Finalize TV Special with Bon Jovi (increase visibility)
- Book fund raisers with my colleagues for my foundation

Strategy — What will make my business successful?
- Global recognition as *Education Feeds Children!* advocate
- Use all contacts to create fund raising opportunities
- Publish articles & get radio interviews
- Contact producer for possible Appalachian documentary

Action — What steps do I need to take?
- Define marketing plan & define my platform by 8/30
- Write minimum 2 articles per month for my blog
- Get my photographer friend to photograph the kids
- 1 hour, 3 days per week to develop social media contacts

Business Plan For _____

Vision
What am I building?

Mission
What is the purpose of my business?

Objectives
What will I measure?

Strategy
What will make my business successful?

Action
What steps do I need to take?

Business Plan For

Chapter Two
What Is This Thing Called Fear?

Too many of us are not living our dreams because we are living our fear.
- Les Brown, author & speaker

Are you tired of leaving your best performance in the studio or practice room? Would you like to change that endless cycle? In this chapter, you will gain clarity on how stage fright affects you. You will realize you have the power to resolve your problem. You may also learn how to identify the source of your fear. Be aware that sometimes the source is very deeply hidden. You may need ghost busters (professional help).

What is performance anxiety?
All of us fear something. For some it's heights, dark places, spiders, and a host of other things. These are phobias. A phobia is an irrational, intense and persistent fear of certain situations, activities, animals, or people. Stage fright too, is a phobia.

When you get up to perform, do you blush, do you sweat, do your knees and hands shake? Are you deafened by anxiety? Is your mind a complete blank when a moment ago you knew all the words? Is your heart beating so fast you can't breathe?

This is a perfect description of how stage fright feels for many people. Some feel all of the symptoms, others a few of them. The fear of public speaking or performing in front of an audience is *Glossophobia* or performance anxiety. People affected with stage fright may be good communicators when talking with their friends, but freeze up on the stage while presenting a talk or performing. It is the most common of all phobias, so you are not alone in your fear.

Do you have mild stage fright or is it severe? Are you completely paralyzed and can't utter a sound? Do you manage to perform but not at the level of which you know you are capable? Is your best simply not available because of the fear? When the fear is beyond one's control, or is interfering with daily life, it takes on the magnitude of an anxiety disorder.

When does the fear begin?
Have you ever seen a baby or a very young child afraid to ask for what it wants? Or afraid to cry when it has needs? No, it's quite the opposite. A child is born with trust and is fearless. Those around the child are the ones that teach the child fear and shame. Most children come into the world with healthy self-esteem. Fear happens with socialization.

However, there are studies that reveal some babies cry when new stimuli are introduced. Other babies are merely curious and not at all upset. The former group may have a genetic predisposition to fear the unknown. Ask your parents or caregivers how you reacted to new things and people. You may learn a great deal. You can't alter your genes but you *can* alter your thought patterns.

Parents and peers

Abusive environments often produce feelings of unworthiness and a lack of confidence, not to mention fear. This negative belief system, if carried into adult life can produce all sorts of unproductive habits including drug addiction, criminal activity and an inability to mold a steady career path.

- Canfield, Hansen, Hewitt, *The Power of Focus*

Unpleasant experiences from childhood create traumas and fears that may remain dormant. They reveal themselves the moment we get up in front of the public and speak or demonstrate some skill we have learned. A child who has experienced humiliation in front of the class by an insensitive teacher may develop stage fright. He or she may not be able to perform or speak well the next time they talk or face a group of people, because of the fear of being humiliated again.

I cannot tell you how many students and colleagues of mine have told me their parents, teachers and friends embarrassed them when they tried to perform. Do any of these comments ring true for you?

- Who gave you the idea you can sing (or play)?
- Stop that noise!
- Put that thing down. You're giving me a headache.
- If you can't do it perfectly, then don't do it at all.
- Rather than make that awful noise, why don't you keep your trap shut?
- Do you really think you have anything of value to say?
- Children should be seen and not heard.
- Thanks dear, that's very nice, but we don't want to hear that right now.
- If you were really so talented, you'd be up there on TV by now.
- You'll never amount to anything.
- If you don't stop crying, I'll give you something to cry about.

These old tapes play when we try to perform or to speak. Feel free to add your own - the list, unfortunately, is endless.

Unconscious imitation

If your parents and relatives are afraid to express themselves, it may have a larger impact than you think. Very timid parents, because of social status or economic strata, may instill a fear mindset by example. I am talking about an attitude of, "I am inferior. I can't speak English the way you can. I don't have your education. I don't have any money therefore I am not worthy of the same respect as you."

We still feel these pressures from our friends, from bosses, from siblings, from families. The old voices that squashed our enthusiasm and our desire to share are still echoing in our unconscious.

Change your present

Even if you are unfortunate enough to have a severely disadvantaged background, you can still make changes. And it may only take one person to help you make the transition. An excellent coach, teacher, therapist, mentor, or positive role model can dramatically impact your future. **The only prerequisite is that you must commit to change.** *When you are ready to do so, the right people will start showing up to help you. In our experience, that well-known saying, "When the pupil is ready, the teacher appears," is true.*

- Canfield, Hansen, Hewitt, The Power of Focus

If any of the statements above make you squirm, a firm decision to transform those old voices into new habits and new patterns is definitely required. Although we can't undo the past, we can change our present and our future. We can change the effect and the power our past holds over us. We can reframe the past and change the stories we tell others and ourselves. By doing so we keep the lesson and let go of the pain.

You need to examine where and when this fear first started. It may be helpful to go to a therapist and work on it. The most important thing for you as an artist and as a human is to do everything in your power to know yourself well. In addition, when you have a situation that is in the way of your creativity, explore as many ways as it takes to resolve the problem. If not, the Ghost of Christmas Past will always lurk in the wings.

Comparison

However, let's not blame everything on parents, peers and social conditioning. What happens when we compare ourselves to other people? This is a very human tendency. For example, if you were a young tenor and you heard Pavarotti sing for the first time and you compared yourself to that incredible sound, you would have come up short.

We all have a tendency, a motivation, to evaluate ourselves – especially in relation to others around us. The belief that you build yourself a valuation based on feedback received from others has validity. That is, if you constantly receive negative feedback without any seeming justification or without any reminder about what was good about your performance, then your self-esteem lowers. If you are told negative things often enough you actually begin to believe them. You do need to be aware of favorable attitudes toward you and your work. The more favorable attitudes are denied you, the more passionately you will wish to hear them. If your self-esteem is low, you will be more likely to hunger for positive feedback. Moreover, you will become even more frustrated and angry if you don't get it. You will respond very positively to good feedback, but you will also respond more despondently to failure then do your colleagues who have high self-esteem. All this all of this in turn, explains how you behave in auditions, why you want approval and why you need to please other people. You want positive feedback.

- Emmons, Thomas, Power Performance for Singers[1]

How you deal with the comparison you feel is telling. Do you give up and throw in the towel? Or do you resolve to be able to perform like the person you are comparing yourself to and get to work?

Personal experience
I know how comparison feels from firsthand experience. There was an elegant, handsome man in my life who was my idol. His name was Josef Ronco. He was an actor, hairdresser, makeup artist – the list goes on - and he changed my life. He told my mother I was an artist when we met. I was two and a half years old! Josef was my first audience. I sang arias for him when I was only seven and he gave me my first acting lessons. Josef told me repeatedly about a magnificent singer named Irene Patti. After I learned a couple of arias, he wanted me to sing for her because she would be able to guide me toward a good teacher.

When I was twelve, my mother and I were at Josef's house for a Christmas party. I was dressed in my holiday best and all excited because I was going to sing for Irene that night. Irene swept into Josef's house dressed to the nines in a gorgeous evening gown. She had just come from singing a concert somewhere with a colleague of hers. They burst into song and Josef's home rang with beauty. I'd never heard an operatic sound live before. It was so gorgeous, so incredibly loud, and so moving! Guess what? I couldn't even say hello. I had completely lost my voice. What a perfect example that it's all in our heads. It's all in our attitude about ourselves.

I was so intimidated by what I perceived, rightfully so, as someone who was so far ahead of me. There was no way I could ever compete with anything that beautiful. It didn't enter my mind that she was a singer in her prime and I was just beginning. Josef helped me see that and Irene became a dear friend and supporter.

Get an education, but perform continuously
Get an education. It is an incredibly valuable thing, for future earning power and the discipline you acquire. Education also teaches you how to learn. *However, you must get out there and perform for people as soon as you can.* Sing, play and perform for anyone who will listen. Dance for the love of it. A bird doesn't sing because it gets applause. It sings because it has a song. Real experience will counteract any ivory tower concepts that may creep in. *There is no experience in any classroom that can top the reality of live performance.*

Performing is essential for performers. Writers must write. No matter how much you learn in a classroom, unless you perform, you are not a performer.

Experiment with different styles
You will find that each style can add a different dimension to your performance. Peter Hofmann was a rock musician before he became a Wagnerian heldentenor. Then he switched to singing musicals and pop songs.

Wynton Marsalis, legendary trumpet player, recorded 10 classical albums and won a Grammy for his first one. He is a musician, composer, educator and co-founded Jazz at Lincoln Center. Variety enriches.

If you want to hear the most amazing switch in styles, listen to soprano Eileen Farrell. Her *Liebestod* from *Tristan und Isolde* is ravishing. Equally authentic and a treat for the ear, is *I've Got a Right to Sing the Blues*, with my great colleague, pianist Ted Taylor. Listen to her

Gershwin interpretations and cabaret song recordings. Yes, it's possible. Don't make yourself so narrow you lose perspective.

In the middle of success
Do you think once you learn how to sing, act, or perform well, that you will become immune to stage fright forever? Nope. Stage fright can creep up on you in the middle of a successful career. It did with Lord Laurence Olivier. This is a great interview on YouTube: watch it. Olivier became so frightened he clung to his *Iago* and stagehands in the wings. He didn't want to go back on stage when he was performing *Othello*. Although he managed to control this fear during the last years of his career, he retreated further and further into character roles where he could mask himself with accents, makeup and disguises. Where did this sudden stage fright come from? Is it something inside of us that realizes "I don't want to do this anymore?" Who knows?

Is there a magic solution?

You don't need to be the best in the world. . .you just need to be the best you can be. And the most natural way to do that is to prepare your body and brain and let them guide you.
   - Michael Colgrass, composer, conductor, Pulitzer Prize and Emmy award winner

Will this book, or a medication or a magic mantra cure your stage fright instantly? The answer is, "No." Controlling stage fright is a process that takes practice. Practice is essential. Without practice nothing will change.

In this book, I will help you honor and strengthen your decision that you alone can change the reality of your present fear. You may be a person who has a gift for performance or you may be just the opposite. You may have had opportunities early in your life to perform and were applauded. Perhaps you performed and were shut down by others.

In either case, the decision to refine your gifts and turn around your weakness is your decision. No one can make that decision for you. No one, no matter how much they care about you, can do the work for you.

Most fine performers were once average and many were terrible. *Many students and performers want to be better but they don't commit to do what it takes.* When you make a firm decision, you will find a shift takes place within and around you. You will suddenly make the time to work on your presentations and performances. You will work in a more focused way. More importantly, you will work on yourself. Opportunities show up that will allow you to showcase what you have been working on. The right people and the right coaches will pop up unexpectedly to help you go forward and reach your goals.

So let's take that resolve, that determination, and go on to find out what you need in your toolbox to achieve your performance goals.

Chapter Two: Summary

Glossophobia is performance anxiety or stage fright.

Most children are born fearless. Phobias develop with socialization. Traumatic childhood experiences may remain dormant until we have to demonstrate something we have learned or speak in public.

We can't undo the past, but we can change our present and our future. We can change the effect, the power, our past holds over us. We can **reframe the past** and **change the stories** we tell others and ourselves. By doing so we keep the lessons, and let go of the pain.

You **need to examine where and when your fear first started**. You may have to go to a therapist or coach to work on it. An artist needs to do everything in their power to know themselves well.

Get an **education, but at the same time, get out there and perform** for people as often as possible.

Experiment with different styles of playing and performing. Variety will give depth to your performances.

Stage fright can creep up at any time.

Controlling stage fright is a process and it takes practice and time. Without practice, nothing will change.

Most fine performers were once average and many were terrible. **Many students and performers want to be better, but they don't commit to do what it takes.**

Chapter Two: Exercises

Instructions: in this section, I want you to write as fast as you can without much thought. If you need another piece of paper, get one, and keep writing.

What have you been told when you perform for people, including family, friends? List the positives & the negatives. Is there a pattern in who voices the negatives? The positives?

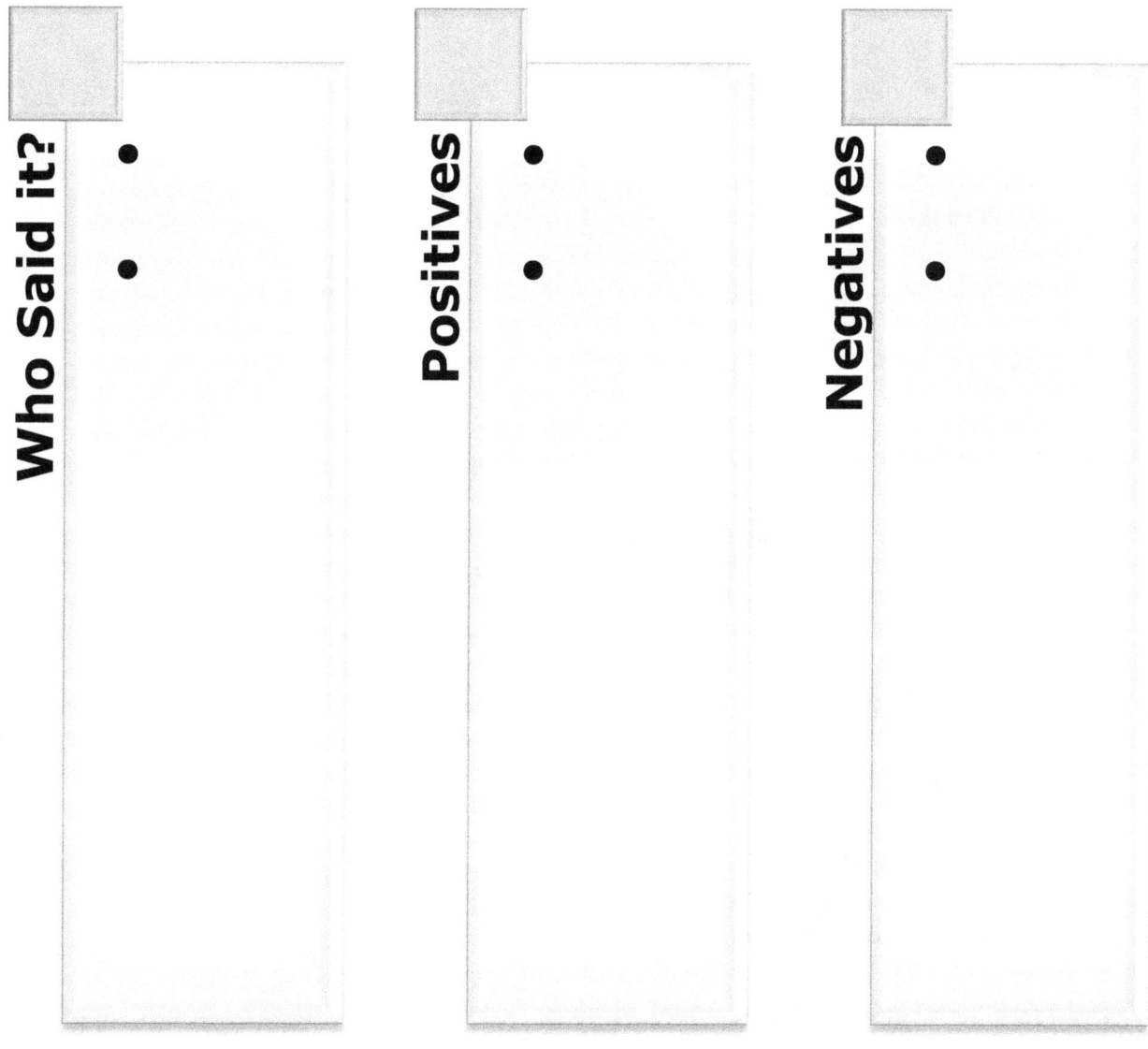

Do you think you have stage fright? If the answer is yes, how does that manifest itself? For example, check those that apply, Add your own body/mind/emotion symptoms in the right column.

☐ SYMPTOMS	☐ YOUR SYMPTOMS
☐ **BODY**	☐
☐ I feel like I will faint	☐
☐ I can't hear	☐
☐ My knees shake	☐
☐ I feel like I'm going to throw up	☐
☐ **MIND**	☐
☐ I feel like I have amnesia	☐
☐ I can't produce what I practiced	☐
☐ I feel embarrassed	☐
☐ I can't get organized	☐
☐ **EMOTIONS**	☐
☐ I feel absolute panic	☐
☐ I feel like I'm not in my body	☐
☐ I feel like a failure	☐
☐ I feel like crying	☐
☐ I feel like a fraud	☐

What is your level of stage fright? Check what best describes you.

- ❏ I feel some excitement in my stomach when I begin.
- ❏ I start shaking when I begin to speak or perform.
- ❏ I feel sick to my stomach.
- ❏ I feel absolute terror and I feel like I'm going to faint.
- ❏ I feel such fear I can't utter a sound.

Is it some combination of these?

What is your greatest fear when you get up to perform?

In reality, what is the worst that has ever happened to you while performing?

What thing or combination of things made you want to perform again?

Can you remember when your stage fright started? Sit quietly and breathe deeply. Was it an event or something that someone said? Was it something your parents said, or your classmates at school, or a tragic event that happened to you? Again, make sure you *do not think about this*, let it rise quickly and write whatever comes to your head no matter how ridiculous it may seem.

What are the negative things you tell yourself? Make a list. Here are three examples:

My Negative Self-Talk	...Continued
I'm going to blow this. I don't really know how to play. My voice will squeak.	

Chapter Three
Performer – Know Thyself

If one man calls you an ass, ignore him.
If two men call you an ass, start looking for tracks.
If three men call you an ass, put on a harness.
- Proverb

Do you know what your strengths are? Your weaknesses? What are you really afraid of? In this chapter, we explore the foundation of it all: self-knowledge. One of the most important keys to conquer an irrational fear like stage fright is to use techniques that help you clarify who you are and what you offer.

Getting to know you
One of the toughest parts about any career as a performer is truly being honest about your abilities. Do you have real ability or is it a desperate need for attention? Have your parents invested in your theatrical and musical education from the time you stood up and sang happy birthday to yourself at your third birthday party? Because of that, do you feel obligated to perform? *Unmet needs control us if we do not drag them out into the sunlight and find a healthy way to feed them.* Get real and get clear before you take action. Learn to listen to your instincts too.

Beware the teacher who always flatters you. Stay away from the coach who says you're the greatest guitarist since Segovia. Why does everyone else make no comment or is curiously unmoved? Whether we like it or not, many people out there are solely motivated to earn money. They are not concerned about how much of a realistic chance you have in the world of performance.

After one of my seminars, a singer asked me about doing a consultation. He wanted a performance evaluation (i.e. development and technique, appearance and voice type and performance readiness). All the while the singer was asking these questions, he kept telling me how supportive his teacher was and how he would not have been able to survive if it hadn't been for his teacher. We scheduled a time. The performer called me and said he had to cancel and take care of a car problem. We scheduled another appointment. He called and told me he lost his ATM card. He had to get another and was unable to withdraw money for the session. The next excuse was that the accompanist was charging too much (it was a standard fee) for an audition. The singer said he would sing with a recording. The session never happened.

Do you notice a pattern? He said he wanted the information. In reality, he was unwilling to hear what everything inside of him already knew. He was too old for his voice type and the roles he desired. His vocal technique was not where it needed to be. He looked his age. He wanted to stay in his make-believe bubble rather than get an evaluation in the real world. That is someone out of touch with reality. They are not professional. They are looking for fame to fulfill their lives. It won't. *Hardcore reality is your friend, not your enemy.*

Hardcore questions

- Do you know the requirements of your particular performance specialty?
- Do you know what your marketplace is looking for now?
- How does your technique measure up to the best in the business?
- What position are you aiming for? (Soloist, ensemble, techie, management).
- How fast do you learn?
- What age do you look? If you are in a branch of the performing arts that is increasingly asking for younger performers, that matters.

If you are aiming for the professional ring, you must be professionally evaluated. Ask not one professional, but several experts who will honestly evaluate your abilities. Sometimes we are hobbled by what we think we *should* want because that's what we've been taught by our family, or by someone who influenced us when we were young. Just because you have natural ability doesn't mean you should pursue a particular avenue of performance. A degree of talent is essential but it is only a small ingredient in the recipe of professional performance success.

The more awareness you have about what you truly love is vital. Love and passion for your work will help generate discipline and evens out the rough spots. That passion is what will get you over the disappointments in this business. Mental toughness will give you the discipline to keep going.

Take the evaluations to heart

Again, *if you are aiming for a professional career, you must go to respected experts to be evaluated.* Go to people who don't have a personal interest in you. Go to dispassionate judges who will tell you, constructively, what they think. In the exercises that follow, you will find indispensable questions that must be answered before you invest another dime in your musical or theatrical career. For many aspiring performers their passion overwhelms reality. You can't – no matter how hard you try – make anyone love you. You can't force a career. Even if you buy your way in, deep inside you will know the truth.

Don't waste another cent of your money and another minute of your precious time working on something for which you do not really have ability, affinity, and a genuine love. That does not mean you are a loser. That simply means you have other talents that are stronger than this one. If you love the cello, but are unable to earn a living in an orchestra, or as a soloist or teacher, then play for your own pleasure. Perspective is also vital: how many spots for star cellists are there?

I'm not saying throw it out. Many of us work at jobs that allow us to have the luxury of sitting on our porch and playing a flute for our own relaxation. There are so many ways to use your gifts to bring other people joy and bring you enormous satisfaction. Play in the park. Play in hospitals. Don't lose the love, but don't pin your hopes on something that is not realistic.

I cannot stress enough how vital it is to know your abilities, talents and shortcomings. If you are a five-foot, size 2 soubrette and your passion is to sing Wagner, you are riding for a fall. If you keep pushing at something for which you are destined to fail because of a lack of ability, you might neglect other abilities and interests that may ignite if fanned by the fire of your attention.

Make the average superior

Are you passionate, committed enough and willing to undergo endless refinements to make the ability you have superlative? If so, you will not only find a slot for yourself, but you will make a position for yourself. In the musical and theatrical industries there are many average talents; but they have enormous drive and incredible technique, which allows them to make a significant mark in the world of entertainment. There are infinite numbers of supremely gifted performers who do not have the mental toughness for a career.

Plan B

I have a student who is very dear to me and whose ability is superlative. His natural equipment far exceeds what you'd expect, even from the best in the business. Yet I tell him: no matter how fabulous you are, no matter how beautifully I guide you, there is no guarantee you will succeed in your passion. There is no guarantee that you will be playing in all the A houses all over the world tomorrow. No matter how hard we work; there is still that funny thing that's out of our control. Call it kismet. Call it fate. Call it whatever you want. Sometimes no matter how hard you work, and with all the gifts you possess, it will not work out for you.

For that reason, I caution all performing artists to have a practical Plan B. Learn the skills of a virtual assistant so you can make your own hours, earn good money, and still schedule auditions. Develop computer skills so you can earn money while you are climbing the ladder. Get a degree in teaching, so when you leave performing, you can slip into a steady career. Learn marketing and use it for own promotion as well. The possibilities are endless.

I don't believe in starving while striving. I did, but if I had other skills to plug in, it might not have been so difficult. *Develop some other revenue-generating interest while you hone your performance skills.* Too many orchestras, opera companies and theaters have disappeared in the past years for you not to heed this warning!

Sometimes, even though you have all the requirements, there may be something deep in your heart that doesn't want you to succeed. Do you feel you are valued only for your performance skills and for the attention it brings those around you? Might that give you an ambivalent view of your success? This is a big question. If it makes you so uncomfortable you want to race over this paragraph, pay special attention to it. This ambivalence leads us to the next question.

Why do you perform?

There's no doubt about it, show business lures the people who didn't get enough love, attention or approval early in life and have grown up to become bottomless, gaping vessels of terrifying, abject need. Please laugh.
- Dennis Miller, American comedian

Do you perform because as a youngster you were patted on the head? Were you applauded as irresistibly cute? Is it your goal to know as much about the oboe as you can because your favorite uncle played? Do you love the idea of sitting in an orchestra, being part of a magnificent whole, rather than a soloist? Is your goal to be a world-class violist or pianist?

Why? I'm asking you to take a very hard look at yourself and ask yourself that question again and again. Each time you ask the question, go deeper. Why am I performing? Most performing artists, actors, singers, instrumentalists or dancers run to the stage like escaping to the circus. For a few magical hours, we are the focus of the most flattering light and attention in the world.

I remember when I learned that. I was about ten years old, attending a concert at an outdoor band shell in Miami. I saw a gorgeous fairy princess on the stage singing a Viennese waltz. I was enchanted. When I saw her afterwards up close, I saw a shoddy old dress, an old, tired face and a badly matched hairpiece. She had applied make-up with a spade and in short, she was anything but a fairy princess. The light man used a bastard amber gel. That amber with a hint of pink warms your face and erases shadows. It can turn an old witch into a princess.

Okay, you have your magical light. You have the rapt attention of an excited audience. You have a place where all of your pain, your anguish, your beauty, your dreams, your power and your rage is applauded. You create characters, colors and moods for the people in the dark who have paid to be entertained. Pretty darned irresistible, isn't it?

The antenna of the race

However, we are far more than illusion. The sensitivity and awareness that makes us an artist is its own reward (and torment). We have the guts to express what is uncomfortable for most humans. *We allow an audience to recognize themselves in us.* That's why they're willing to pay money to sit in the dark and cry, laugh, and experience the extremes of emotion they are afraid to touch. Virginia Woolf called artists the "antenna of the race," and we are. We interpret and translate our present world. That is quite a privilege and quite a responsibility. Oscar Wilde in *The Picture of Dorian Gray* expressed what an artist could do perfectly:

If this girl can give a soul to those who have lived without one, if she can create the sense of beauty in people whose lives have been sordid and ugly, if she can strip them of their selfishness and lend them tears for sorrows that are not their own, she is worthy of all your adoration, worthy of the adoration of the world.[1]

The magic of sharing

I promise you there is a place inside of you that has to do with sharing, not selling. It can transform your performance level. The methods in this book will help that transformation. Increasing your self-knowledge will help, but the sharing is something you must come to on your own. When your cry becomes not, "Look at me, look at me!" but instead, "I'm so excited about this, I can't wait to share it with you," a new world will open before your eyes.

Picture an excited child playing in the sun. They run to you with a handful of M&Ms, "Want some?" Do you think the child is worried the candies are melting or they may have sand on them? No. They are sharing a treasure with someone they love. When you find that feeling, you will walk into what Abraham Maslow called self-actualized flow.

Abraham Maslow described self-actualization as using all of our talents, capabilities and potential in an ongoing process of becoming all we can be. As performers, aren't we seeking the very same things? Self-actualized people see life more clearly. They are more objective and less likely to allow hopes, fears, or ego defenses to distort their view of life. Maslow found that most self-actualizing people are dedicated to a vocation or to a cause, not merely performing a job. Again, those same qualities define an artist. The catalyst that ignites all of these qualities is joy. When we as performers can contact that irrepressible joy that can't be affected by our outer world, we are beginning to touch the essence of artistic creation.

When our hungry ego evolves into an artist who has honed his or her craft into mastery, then it's a pleasure to be on stage. It's a privilege to share your interpretation of a moment in time, and it can be intoxicating. A voice actor may discover the core of a character's voice, a cellist a legato phrase that soars. A pianist shivers a Chopin trill and a dancer tattoos a flamenco rage. The sylph-like arms of a ballerina or an actor may contact the power of baring their soul.

Finding that kind of vision, understanding and beauty shared is a very powerful tool for eliminating fear. It defeats fear, because your focus becomes not perfection, but the deep joy of superb communication.

What are you afraid of?

I think it's important to ask yourself this question. What is the worst-case scenario that plays in your head? Is it that you're going to be humiliated and everyone will laugh at you? Is it that you're going to blow this audition so bad they'll never ask you back? Will you forget everything you've learned? Will your technique fly right out the window and you'll stand there, paralyzed? Well, all of these things could happen. And you know something? The world is not going to stop. We've all done it and the world continues to turn.

If you blow an audition or performance, one of the most important things you can do, as soon as possible, is go to your teacher and analyze the performance in depth. Athletes do it. Why not us? You must list the positives as well as the negatives. We will talk about this in more detail later in the book. That 'after' analysis is very important. It is as important as the 'before' preparation. *If you don't know what you did wrong, you are more than likely to repeat those same mistakes again.*

Fail better

Ever tried. Ever failed. No matter. Try again, fail again. Fail better.
- Samuel Beckett, Irish author, dramatist

This is the time for you to take a serious, nonjudgmental appraisal of what happened and how to prevent that same thing from happening again. Use the worst-case scenario as a way to make thorough preparation. For example, if you're relying on public transportation, there could be a break down in the subway or the buses. Make sure you start out two hours earlier. If you're driving, you could have a flat tire.

What about using that same hypersensitive imagination to create a best-case scenario and prepare for that as well? How about imagining an exciting performance that carries you and your audience to another level? I remember coming down impossibly shallow steps in a new production of *Samson et Dalila* in Australia. I had visualized my entrance in such detail I am convinced it saved me from disaster. I was coming down steps too narrow for my feet and covered with slippery fake grass. I locked eyes with Samson and floated down letting rose petals drift out of my hands. I slipped on the last step and almost fell flat on my face. But I was not going to allow anything to disturb the magic of the spell we had so carefully created. I managed to keep floating right onto the stage and into the first notes of the aria. It happened as I visualized it. And yes, I had a very strong physical core to support myself.

Personal experience

Is there ever a time that no matter what you do, you will be nervous? Yes, it happens. Back in the early 1980s Peter Brook had created a new version of Bizet's *Carmen*. I was very excited because my agent at Columbia Artists (CAMI) got me an audition for the production. I remember I dressed very simply, comfortably and appropriately. I walked into the audition room and saw not only Peter Brook, but also an agent known for making or breaking careers. One of my dear friends had told me repeatedly I needed to sing for this man. If he liked me, it could make a difference in the entire trajectory of my career.

I didn't feel ready to audition for him yet and had repeatedly put it off. My friend wasn't exaggerating: this man had indeed designed and fostered several careers. I panicked. I became so nervous I was shaking. My voice was shaking and my knees were shaking. I couldn't breathe and I couldn't sing. I think I sang the *Seguidilla*. I really don't remember. Peter Brook asked me to sing the *Card Aria*. In my desperation to get over my terror, I knelt on the stage. His question to me was, "So, do you always do things the same way?" I don't remember how I sang the aria. I'm sure I sang badly. I did not get the part.

Now comes the fun part - 20/20 hindsight. What would I have done now? Remember, this is my hindsight and it is very subjective. You may have a different take on this situation. The right answer is the one that works for you. First, I would have been honest. If my honesty would have lost me the audition, okay. That was better than to try to push through and fake it. I might have said, "Please forgive me. I'm awfully nervous. I just need to breathe. May I get some water?" I would have walked out, calmed myself with belly breathing, gone back in and asked Peter Brook, "Will you please direct me? I know I will get calmer." Maybe it would have worked, maybe not.

All I can say is, you will have times like this. My career didn't end. I sang quite successfully for another twenty years. Might my career have taken another, more successful, path? Maybe. No matter how well you prepare, unexpected situations will arise. All you can do is hook into your mental toughness. Pick yourself up, brush yourself off and start all over again. Yes, it's a song.

There is also an appropriate martial arts motto for this occasion. Fall down seven times get up eight. And if you want to feel a lot better go to the next chapter.

Chapter Three: Summary

One of the most important ways to conquer an irrational fear like stage fright is to **clarify who you are and what you offer**. Get real.

If you are aiming for a professional career, **go to several respected professionals to evaluate your abilities**. Go to people who have no personal interest in you.

A degree of **talent is essential, but only a small ingredient** in the recipe of professional performance success.

The more awareness you have about what you truly love is important because **love and passion for your work is the thing that generates discipline** and softens the rough spots.

Don't lose the love, but **don't pin your hopes on something that is not realistic**. If you keep pushing at something at which you are destined to fail because of a lack of ability, you may neglect other interests that will bring you greater rewards.

In the performance industries, **average talents with enormous drive and incredible technique have made a mark in the world of entertainment**. There are also **supremely gifted performers who do not have the mental toughness for a career**.

Ask yourself many times, **"Why am I performing?"**

Think of **performing as sharing a treasure with someone you love**, or explaining something you love, to someone you care about.

The world is not going to stop if you blow an audition or a performance. This is not brain surgery.

The quality of your 'after' analysis is as important as the 'before' preparation. If you don't know what you did wrong, you are more likely to repeat the same mistakes again.

Fall down seven times get up eight.

Chapter Three: Exercises

What are your strengths?

What is the level of your talent? Is it of such quality or obvious potential that everyone who hears you is astounded? Are your piano, voice, acting, conducting, or instrumental skills so superlative that everyone who witnesses a performance is flabbergasted, and wants you to sign a contract?

If at least three respected professionals in your field agree you are extraordinary, then the next questions don't have as much weight as they do for the more ordinarily gifted performer. Don't be insulted. How many voices are there like Pavarotti? How many cellists like Yo-Yo Ma, how many conductors like Leonard Bernstein? Having great gifts still requires training, discipline, and refining, but there will be more people interested in helping you achieve your goals.

Remember too, there are many performers who began with average talent, but who had such passion and devotion for their work, they rose to prominence in their chosen professions, no matter the odds.

Your reply:

Are you open to learning and absorbing new material? Have you developed skills for rapid learning? Do you have a method for memorization and are able to digest and perform new material quickly? Are you an excellent sight-reader or do you need more time to learn your music? Are you able to learn dialogue and take direction quickly and easily?

Your reply:

Are you a physical type desirable in a theatrical career? This is especially true of opera, musical comedy and the world of straight theater. It's important that we look the part. Are you 47 years old and ready to audition for the young ingénue lead? You are setting yourself up for failure. In the world of instrumental music, appearance is not quite as exacting, but managers today would prefer to have a sax player who is sexy and attractive. It makes their marketing job easier. I didn't say this business was fair, did I?

Your reply:

Is your voice type, or your instrument of choice needed in the professional world of music, dance and theater? Where is it needed? When one finds a ringing Heldentenor, there is always a niche for them, the same for the low contralto. Are you a jazz pianist with great arranging skills? *You need to know yourself and what you offer.* Are there 20 superstar pianists making the rounds of the big orchestras? If so, you better have three hands to succeed!

Your reply:

Is your personal life conducive to developing a musical or theatrical career? If you are the mother of young children, it is not easy to concentrate on repertoire as someone without those responsibilities. Do you have parents, sponsors or a spouse who can help? Don't forget, you need not only the money, but the time, to devote to your musical or theatrical refinement.

Your reply:

Do you have enough ambition and discipline to pursue an evasive, unpredictable goal? You might be tremendously fortunate, and rise to the desired level of your profession two years after breaking into the professional scene. I assure you that's very rare. Are you willing to do what it takes to refine your gifts to a level of extreme professionalism? Even with no guarantee that the work will bring you success enough to maintain a comfortable life?

Your reply:

Do you have the mental toughness to succeed? Having assessed your true abilities, are you willing to commit to making them the best they possibly can be? Are you willing to commit to the mental discipline that will allow you to function under the most difficult of circumstances?

Your reply:

If the majority of the answers to these questions is negative, performance may not be for you. You may have other abilities you have ignored because the siren call of the limelight was too strong.

I know from experience my point of view is realistic. However, there are those performers that succeed against all odds. No matter how illogical it seems, they succeed and they rise to the top.

Awareness of your existing reality is essential to your success. I wish for you to find joy in the refining of your gift. If there is no joy (since most of the time is spent refining and a relatively small amount of time performing), you need to ask yourself if your heart is fulfilled by the journey, not just the destination.

No matter how you decide to use your artistic gifts, you are the antenna of the race, and your artistic sensitivity is needed on this planet. *Whether or not you make a living on the stage, the greatest work of art you will ever create is your own life.*

Notes:

Questions for your evaluators
They may not answer all of these questions directly, or you may choose to make a questionnaire with fewer or more questions. They may instead prefer to sit and talk with you and answer questions. You will more than likely have paid a fee for their services: use them to the fullest.

Use this sheet as a guide to ask questions if they don't want to write things down. This way you have a form to fill out for yourself.

Name/contact information	Scoring 1-5 (5 is the highest)
Level of talent.	
Technical skills. Ready for the professional arena? Now? When?	
Physical type. Does my physicality and appearance match my type and is it theatrically appealing?	
Demand for voice type/ instrument/ dancer/actor	
Mental toughness. What is your impression?	
Comments:	

Evaluation Sheet (Score 1-5, 5 is Highest)

Name/contact information	Scoring 1-5 (5 is the highest)
Level of talent.	
Technical skills. Ready for the professional arena? Now? When?	
Physical type. Does my physicality and appearance match my type and is it theatrically appealing?	
Demand for voice type/ instrument/ dancer/actor	
Mental toughness. What is your impression?	
Comments:	

The Mental Toughness Quiz

Directions: Make one choice for each question. Pick the closest answer to how you feel. Use the number of the question as the score you get for that question, i.e. If you pick answer number two to question A, my score is 2 for question A.

A. **Why do you perform?**
   1. Because I just have to. I'd pop if I didn't!
   2. I like it more than anything else I've tried.
   3. I have an exceptional ability for this.
   4. Everybody loves it when I perform, and I have a lot of fun.
   5. My mother (replace with appropriate person) loves when I perform.

B. **How does the act of performing make you feel?**
   1. It's an incredible high!
   2. I really like it.
   3. It makes me nervous, but I still like it.
   4. It makes people like me.
   5. What was I thinking?

C. **How do you like the preparation for performance?**
   1. I love the rehearsal more than the performance.
   2. I love the end result, so I do it.
   3. It's hard, but it makes me less nervous when I do it.
   4. It's okay, but it's a necessary evil.
   5. What preparation?

D. **How much time do you spend on mental preparation?**
   1. 15 minutes per day.
   2. 10 minutes per day for sure, longer if I can.
   3. Sometimes I do 5 minutes, sometimes not.
   4. None, my technique is what counts.
   5. What do you mean by that?

E. **How important is dress rehearsal to you?** Dress rehearsal, as defined by a full out rehearsal with a real audience or an imaginary one, dressed for the occasion and with all the advance preparation necessary.
   1. So important – I need it to do well
   2. Important, takes a lot of time, but it's worth it.
   3. I make time for at least one dress rehearsal.
   4. Yeah, it's important, but I don't have the time.
   5. I don't really think it's important.

F. **What does constructive criticism do for you?**
    1. Great, it guides me to be my best.
    2. Like it, but it takes a lot of time to incorporate.
    3. Okay, but that person needs to be really careful. I get hurt.
    4. Okay, but confuses me. Doesn't my teacher always know best?
    5. Criticism is criticism, I don't like it.

G. **Do you think it's important to take time off from your work?**
    1. Well, since even the Lord rested, I think so!
    2. I'm getting better at taking some time off.
    3. It's tough, but even five minutes in an hour makes a difference in my practice.
    4. I don't like time off. I get lazy.
    5. Why do I need time off? My technique isn't good enough yet.

H. **How important is relaxation in performance?**
    1. It's essential!
    2. Relaxation allows me to do my best.
    3. Relaxation is a good thing, I don't do it enough.
    4. Relaxation confuses me. I need energy.
    5. Relaxation is a six-pack on the beach.

I. **How important to your career is your look and appearance?**
    1. It's part of my brand, very important.
    2. It makes me feel good, one less thing to worry about.
    3. Important, and I need to be very comfortable.
    4. Haven't got the money for designer duds.
    5. My appearance has nothing to do with my performance.

J. **How important is punctuality and preparedness in your career?**
    1. It's everything, if you're not – it gets around.
    2. I like being on time, and knowing my stuff – it feels better.
    3. It's good, but sometimes I don't know my material yet.
    4. I know my stuff, but public transportation is tricky.
    5. Marilyn Monroe was always late and they waited for her.

K. **Do you understand what "Fall down seven times, get up eight" means?**
    1. Yes
    2. No

L. **You need a lot of money to be a successful artist.**
    1. Not if you have extraordinary talent and drive.
    2. Not necessarily, there are scholarships and grants available.
    3. Yes

M. **How important are *your* marketing efforts to your career?**
    1. Without it, I'm sunk.
    2. Real important, I'm responsible for my success.
    3. Important, but oh, the time it takes!
    4. Let my agent do it, that's what I pay them for.
    5. It has nothing to do with my art.

N. **You'll be happy when you become a star.**
    1. Not necessarily, happiness is my choice.
    2. Maybe, sounds good, but risky to pin all my hopes on that.
    3. I will feel good, but especially to be respected by my colleagues.
    4. Things will change when I'm a star.
    5. You bet – power, riches – can't wait!

O. **Do you need to be a star to be a successful performer?**
    1. No, I want to be the best I can be.
    2. No, if I can make a good living at what I love I'll be happy and lucky.
    3. Maybe, but I want to be a respected professional.
    4. Don't know, ask me in five years.
    5. Well, yeah, if not, what's the point?

Scoring the mental toughness quiz

I hope you were absolutely honest in answering these questions. Nobody is grading you. The results of this quiz will help you understand more about mental toughness. Not only that, you will get clear about what you truly believe, and what you may have to adjust and change.

15 to 25 points	**You have a handle on mental toughness.** You understand what it is and have a very realistic idea of what a career in show business involves. Keep walking; you've got a very good chance of success.
25 to 35 points	**Good work.** You get it. Keep sharpening your skills and maintain your focus. Success is built step by step.
35 to 45 points	**You are most certainly on the right track.** Keep going and walk from illusion into reality. Hard-core reality is your friend. Find out what aspect of this business you love, design a plan to get there, and go for it - full steam ahead!
45 to 55 points	**You're doing okay,** but I want more than okay for you. I imagine you do, too. Work on the exercises in this book, keep developing your skills, from marketing to business, not just your talent. Get real, get clear, get going!
55 to 65 points	**Let's rethink this plan.** Start reading some biographies about the greats in your field. Even if you have extraordinary talent, you need mental toughness to get where you want to go. Sharpen those skills and stay focused.
65 to 70 points	**You need to revise your idea of mental toughness.** Your concepts of why you perform, preparation and criticism need a major overhaul. If the desire is there to learn, implement what's in this book, and your horizons will widen.

Chapter Four
Do Drugs -- You'll Feel Much Better, or Not

In sports, there are very clear-cut rules about drugs. There are no such stringent rules for performers and artists on the stage. There would be more stringent regulations if Nike was sponsoring musicians the way athletes are supported.
  - Dr. Charles Yesalis, Professor Emeritus, Pennsylvania State University

> **WARNING:** I am not a medical doctor and I'm not making any suggestions to take drugs, prescription or otherwise. Even herbs and homeopathic medicines can harm you. If you have an allergic or medical condition, you could die from anaphylactic shock (breathing passages and tongue can swell). I am simply mentioning possible resources that you might explore with the help of a doctor or a licensed professional.

There are two different schools of thought on using medication to enhance, and in some cases, even permit, performance. Sara Sant'Ambrogio, the cellist in the magnificent Eroica trio says, "If you have to take a drug to do your job then go get another job." Barry Green, author of *The Inner Game of Music*, brands chemically assisted performances as soulless and inauthentic.[1] What do you think? Perhaps neither of them have ever experienced the terror of stage fright.

Are there other ways of dealing with stage fright? Are there chemical substances that can help? Do you have allergies? Are you troubled by GERD? In striving for first class artistry, we are looking for an Olympic level of performance. As you know, in sports you are dropped from competition if you are found to use certain kinds of drugs.

As a musician, your body is an extension of your instrument. As a singer, dancer or actor, your body *is* your instrument. I am simply touching on this huge subject so that you as a performing artist can explore options that may be of help. Please do so carefully. In the exercises, I share some of my favorite performance remedies. Experiment responsibly and get professional medical advice.

Aromatherapy
With the increasing demand for holistic health care and the green revolution, the demand for aromatherapy will increase. . . It will become routine for doctors to send culture samples to the pharmacist for testing, and identify the relevant aromatherapy for the patient. The stress-relieving properties associated with aromatherapy make it an indispensable part of health care.
  - Robert Tisserand, international aromatherapy expert

In spite of my desire to remain neutral, I admit I am prejudiced in favor of the least invasive help for performers' ills available. Fragrance is such an integral part of our lives. Smells of childhood, good or bad, evoke feelings. I used to carry *Nag Champa* incense all over the world to transform hotels rooms into a bit of home. This is my preferred method of invoking calm. It's non-invasive, safe, free of side effects and doesn't affect my technique in any way.

It's practical magic. Doesn't a whiff of baking bread bring back positive memories? Why do you think realtors bake cookies when they have an open house? It works.

My preferred performance aid is aromatherapy. My favorite over the years has been lavender oil. A few drops of concentrated lavender is wonderfully soothing, but make sure it's real. So many oils are artificial and can actually give you a headache. Lavender oil quiets the nervous system and can even help you fall asleep.

Make your own potions. You can buy a good quality neutral, unscented lotion and add the essential oils you love. It's less expensive and totally yours! Be very careful of applying essential oils to your skin. They are concentrated and can irritate. Experiment with what works for you. If you use a fragrance in your pre-performance ritual, you can invoke the same calm and prepared state you're looking for when you are on stage.

If you are onstage in a press of people make sure your colleagues are not allergic to the scent. Check that out beforehand.

Aromatherapy – the negative kind

There is a different sort of aromatherapy that can be most un-therapeutic. When a person is smoking, even if they're at a great distance from you in an enclosed room or even outside, don't you smell their smoke? Isn't what you smell not just their smoke, but also their breath? Please, please have consideration for your colleagues. Take a bath and use deodorant. Some of the horrible old costumes we actors have to wear smell bad enough! Oral hygiene is of paramount importance. Brush your teeth and floss. Go to a dentist and get your teeth cleaned periodically. It's not just considerate: it's essential for your good health.

Homeopathic remedies

Homeopathic remedies are also popular because of their relative lack of side effects. However, they can lose their effectiveness with certain foods, drink, herbs and other medications. Homeopathy is based on the idea that like can cure like. Disease can be treated by extremely diluted doses of drugs that produce symptoms of the disease in healthy people. Sound strange? I have used many homeopathic remedies and they work for me.

There are many homeopathic remedies available to alleviate stage fright and its symptoms. There are many solutions for digestive upset. In the US at stores like Whole Foods, some drugstores and most natural food stores, you can get advice and beneficial products.

Read instructions thoroughly and do your research. Never – NEVER - take any remedy or medication without having tried it in rehearsal first.

The thirty-eight Bach Flower Remedies are very gentle and effective homeopathic remedies to explore. I always kept *Rescue Remedy*, an ideal mix for stress, in my theater kit.

Your best bet of course, is to have your remedies tailored for you by a homeopathic practitioner. For short-term use relief is at hand if used as directed. With homeopathic remedies, allow at least twenty minutes before you eat or drink anything. These tiny pills or drops are dissolved under your tongue, rather than swallowed with water. Don't take them if you just brushed your teeth, or ate. Your mouth needs to be clean.

Follow the directions on the container. Again I caution, do not use any of these remedies for the first time at a performance. You need to use them, or experiment with them, at rehearsals. Even something as gentle as the Bach flower remedies or aromatherapy needs experimentation to see how it works for you.

An invaluable over-the-counter remedy is ordinary saline solution. We all need saline for our mucous membranes and for survival. Whether you travel or not, this is a lifesaver in a bottle. I'm not just talking to singers. How well can you play a sax with a stuffed up nose? One of the best ways of avoiding infection during flu season is to use saline solution in your nose. It allows the membranes in your nose to be moist instead of dry and susceptible to germs. Have you ever inhaled salt water while swimming in the ocean? It clears out your sinuses doesn't it? Try a Neti pot: it's gentler than the ocean. My favorite bottled saline is Ayr. The brand makes drops and a nasal saline gel that clings to the inside of your nose and keeps you moistened. Absolutely invaluable. You will be amazed at the results.

Alcohol
I have to admit I am passionately against combining alcohol and performance, but to ignore it would be unrealistic. Many "I'll just have a quick sip of vodka," has turned into a drunken member of the wedding party ruining not just his speech, but a best friend's wedding. How many instances are there of a mix of alcohol and performance creating disastrous results? It's one of the easiest substances available for self-medication, but decidedly risky. Alcohol's downside is far more potent than the relief.

For a singer or actor, it packs a negative quadruple whammy. We need moisture in our mouths, throats, and our nasal cavities. Alcohol has the opposite effect: it dries us out. It impairs our awareness, and coordination. Most of all, it impairs our judgment.

Herbal Remedies
Herbal remedies are also helpful. For example, valerian and catnip are good choices as they both calm and relieve anxiety. Too much and you will go to sleep. However, with anything we ingest, side effects are possible and long-term use could be a problem. Do your research. In addition, when you dull your senses, you are also dulling your technical execution. I personally feel that any substance that interferes with our motor functions interferes with top-flight performance.

Chamomile tea can be very soothing.. I drank chamomile, but found out later, I was allergic to it. It made my sinuses swell. If you have tree and grass allergies, you may be more susceptible to certain herbs. There are many herbs to help reflux. Try peppermint tea or capsules before you take pills for GERD. Experiment and find out which foods you need to avoid.

Herbals teas can be used in tea infusers, also called tea balls. You fill them with loose tea, screw them closed and let them steep: it's greener and no teabags or tags for the landfill. Also at many health food stores you can get loose, dried herbs more cheaply than packaged teas.

> **Warning:** Many of these herbs, liquids or potions you take with you may create problems at airports. When I was taking allergy shots, I had to carry my prescription along with my serums and syringes. Even with a doctor's note, I had to explain. Be prepared and allow more time to get through security.

Other helpful options

Aside from pills and potions there are very valuable modalities to help a performer in their career health. **Massage** is invaluable. There are so many different types; simple stroking to deep tissue to shiatsu to Thai massage. The Thai monk who taught me what evolved into the *Cycle of Nine* treated a roofer who was crippled and unable to walk from injuries he received when he fell on the job site. At first, for two years he was carried to the monastery to be treated by the monk. Later he came with two canes until after 6 years of treatment he was able to walk unaided. Massage can be that miraculous!

Therapy, counseling and **professional coaching** can transform your career path and your life. They can help unlock blockages and spur you on to new heights.

Yoga and **exercise** make for supple, energetic performance. I always did yoga before my performances. It saved me from injury and made me strong and flexible. **Chiropractic** can offer relief from injuries and align us for better performance.

Meditation is invaluable for quieting our monkey minds and preparing us for excellence. The options are abundant – use them.

Food as Medicine

Yes, food is medicine. Think about this. We spend so much money on our houses and where we live and yet we balk at the horrible prices of fresh and organic food. Well, *your real house is the body you live in!* And as an athlete (performers are athletes) you need to take care of your body. If you feel well, your interaction with the outside world will improve. You will become an agent for positive change on this planet. That can be your longest running, most profitable role for you.

I found I had a world of allergies. I was allergic to wheat (that is gluten, bread, pasta etc.), dairy, mold, dust; the list was endless. When I took shots and got off of the allergens, my symptoms vanished and my energy soared. We really are what we eat. Whenever I gained weight, it was because I wasn't eating properly. Your health is in your hands.

Prescription Options

Beta blockers are used widely in musical performance to ease stage fright and performance anxiety. There are of course two camps. One side says the drugs are a godsend and the other says it's a crutch. I was afraid of utilizing any drugs that might get in the way of my performance so I didn't use them. I suspected my inspiration or my fire would be dampened.

Beta blockers are cardiac medications. They are not tranquilizers or sedatives and are used for disorders like abnormal heart rhythms, high blood pressure and angina. They block the action of adrenaline. Adrenaline causes a fight or flight response to any perceived danger – from a charging mama grizzly to a Blue Note audience.

Is it illegal? Dangerous?
The bad news is that a large percentage of musicians and performers who take beta blockers get them from friends and not physicians. Others buy them while touring in countries where they're sold over the counter. You are taking a risk when a physician does not prescribe the drugs.

Beta blockade enhances pulmonary, cardiovascular, and dermatologic and organ effects of mediators and increases mortality associated with experimental anaphylaxis induced by either immunologic or non-immunologic mechanisms.[3]

> **Let's put that into English. Beta blockers can be dangerous if you have asthma or heart disease. Beware of doing any allergy skin testing while taking them. It can be deadly.**

Beta blockers, or performance *enablers*, are not illegal if a doctor prescribes them. Performance *enhancers* are often obtained illegally. There are rules in sport and competition that specify no performance enhancers. You risk disqualification if you use prohibited substances. In archery, for example, even a performance enabler like a beta blocker is looked on as an unfair advantage. A shooter using beta blockers can take a more precise shot in between heartbeats.

In sports, there are very clear-cut rules. There are no such stringent rules for performers and artists on the stage. Dr. Charles Yesalis, Professor Emeritus at Pennsylvania State University, brought up a good point when he said there would be more stringent regulations if Nike was sponsoring musicians the way athletes are supported.

Performance enhancers and enablers
Dr. Yesalis, a leading expert on drug use in performance, worked primarily with athletes in his long career. He did scientific research on the use and abuse of performance enhancing substances in sport and exercise. He testified before Congress on legislation dealing with the control of anabolic steroids and growth hormones. He appeared before the US Senate Judiciary Committee and the Drug Enforcement Administration. Dr. Yesalis worked closely with the NFL Players Association, FDA, Centers for Disease Control and Prevention, US Olympic Committee, National College Athletic Association and the National Strength and Conditioning Association.

He is the author or co-author on authoritative books on steroids. The most recent, *The Steroids Game*, focuses on education, prevention and intervention of anabolic steroid use in athletics. Dr. Yesalis is a well-known speaker and he told me he begins most of his talks with this comment: "It is innate in man to try to gain an advantage. That's simply the way we humans are made. To ignore that fact is to be extremely naïve." Dr. Yesalis states that since recorded history, athletes in competition have used food and other substances to be stronger and faster than their opponents. This is not a new concept.

What does this have to do with an artist? What do an athlete and a performer have in common? In my opinion, *an athlete is a performer and a performer is an athlete.* In the same way that an athlete knows their body and knows what makes them perform best, we, as performers, have exactly the same responsibility. Those in the elite circle have enormous self-knowledge.

In our conversation, Dr. Yesalis agreed there is a difference between performance *enhancers* such as anabolic steroids, and performance *enablers* such as beta blockers, corticosteroids and anti-inflammatory drugs. A performance enhancer, (for example caffeine, one of the legal enhancers) makes your performance better. For the purposes of this book, I am primarily discussing performance enablers.

A performance enabler allows you to perform. In other words, if you are hoarse and unable to sing, a doctor may prescribe cortisone. Over my long career, there were half a dozen times when, without steroids, I would not have been able to sing. Afterwards I had to be quiet and allow the vocal cords to return to normal and the effects of the drugs to wear off. A beta blocker is in the category of an enabler. Without it, you may not be able to perform. I read of a flautist who wished for at least studio level performance on stage. Instead, nerves destroyed her peace of mind so intensely and her hands would sweat so much, she couldn't hold the flute. After a doctor prescribed beta blockers she was able to play.

If we think about the comment, *'If you need to take pills get another job,'* we have a quandary. We have made so many advances in the types of drugs that are now available, as well as new and more subtle uses of these drugs. What would it have meant to his public if Glenn Gould, the incredible pianist, had taken carefully monitored doses of these modern miracles? He only performed 200 public concerts in his entire career because of his stage fright. Van Cliburn performed 200 times in only a couple of seasons. Gould retreated to the recording studio. Maybe with the right kind of meds and the right kind of dosing, more people could have experienced this genius live.

Again, there is no black and white answer to this question. What works for you? Don't experiment casually with your health. Think like an elite athlete. Know your instrument, your body, thoroughly. Learn what works for you.

Dr. Yesalis suggested that I watch a film called *Bigger, Stronger, Faster*. It is a film primarily about the use of performance enhancers such as anabolic steroids. I highly recommend the film. It tracks the journey of three brothers from New York who wanted to make it big in bodybuilding and WWF. The wrestling network rejected the older brother several times. They said he was too old and not what they were looking for. He was only 36 and had been taking anabolic steroids for most of his life. He moved out to California to become famous and work out at Gold's Gym. You can see in the interview that nothing else mattered in his life except to succeed in wrestling. The sadness and sense of defeat in his wife's face is heartbreaking. He felt he had no worth unless he achieved that fame. It didn't happen. A year after the film was released, he died. I cannot tell you how many performers I have seen with that same unhealthy obsession. *Fame will not make you happy. Only you can make you happy.*

The rare 1%
Dr. Yesalis also commented on a fascinating group of people. Over the years, he has learned there is a remarkable group of 1% of elite athletes who get out there on the field (or the stage) and surpass themselves repeatedly. That is a unique and singular personality type and a gift. Most of us don't have it. These rare few like the hockey great Wayne Gretsky, thrive on the roar of the greasepaint and the smell of the crowd. They feed on the excitement. They are excited and inspired by the people cheering them on. We ordinary mortals are not in that small percentile of the rare. We have to find other ways of dealing with nerves, fear, physical ailments and poor preparation. If you're in that one percentile you probably don't need this book.

You miss 100% of the shots you never take.
- Wayne Gretsky, hockey great

A club for shy souls
Something infinitely more fun than taking drugs is a creative solution. This was the brainchild of a concert pianist in New York during World War II. He began a self-help group he dubbed, The Society for Timid Souls. When I discovered this fascinating story in my research for this book, I was delighted with the idea. He held meetings in his apartment. Performers who had problems with stage fright would perform for the members of this club. While they were performing, the members of the society would boo and make noise, have conversations and in general, harass the performer, until eventually, the performer became immune to what bothered them. When they actually performed in public most normal audiences were probably quite mild compared to the performers' colleagues in The Society for Timid Souls.

This concept is called desensitization (like taking allergy shots). I know it also helps to get into the venue where you are going to perform and spend some time just being there. I used to lie on the stage looking up at the lights before a performance. I felt, with all of my senses, the history in the boards and renewed my vow to always do my best. Don't you think that's a romantic notion for such a realist? There has to be some magic.

The debate goes on
I don't have an answer to the question of drugs. This is an overview of some of the resources and solutions available. My solution to performance anxiety was to use the natural avenues of aromatherapy and homeopathy. My experimentation with performance enhancers was limited to caffeine when I was exhausted and acupuncture. I was afraid beta blockers would affect my performance. Find out what works for you. Approach anything you ingest with extreme caution and with professional help.

Now you have a guide to some of the medicinal and creative solutions available to soothe your fear. What about the people waiting to experience the magic you have to offer? Are the people in the dark your enemy? Are most audiences hostile? If you think so, let us find a way to change your perception.

Chapter Four: Summary

> **WARNING:** I am not a medical doctor and I'm not making any suggestions to take drugs, prescription or otherwise. Even herbs and homeopathic medicines can harm you. If you have an allergic or medical condition, you could die from anaphylactic shock (breathing passages and tongue swell). I am simply mentioning possible resources that you might explore with the help of a doctor or a licensed professional.

Aromatherapy uses fragrance to affect your mood and state of mind. It can help you achieve clarity and relaxation.

Homeopathic remedies are based on the idea that like can cure like. Disease can be treated by extremely diluted doses of drugs that produce symptoms of the disease in healthy people.

Alcohol is drying, can be addictive and deadly to the coordination necessary for excellent performance.

Herbal remedies can relieve anxiety. They can also put you to sleep or poison you. Do your research. And remember, when you dull your senses, you are also dulling your technical execution. If you have tree and grass allergies, you may be more susceptible to certain herbs.

Warning: many of these herbs, liquids, or potions you carry may create problems at airports. When I was taking allergy shots, I had to carry my prescription along with my serums and syringes. Even with a doctor's note, I had to explain – so be prepared.

Prescription options: Beta blockers are cardiac medications. They are not tranquilizers or sedatives. Go to a doctor and be assessed before you take a medication of this sort. If you have asthma or heart disease, be aware of doing any allergy skin testing while taking beta blockers. It can be deadly.

There is no black and white answer to the debate of taking drugs or not. What works for you? **Don't experiment casually with your body.** Think like an elite athlete. Know your instrument thoroughly.

Read instructions thoroughly and do your research. **Never – NEVER - take any remedy or medication without having tried it in rehearsal first.**

Your best bet is to have your remedies tailored for you by a homeopathic practitioner or herbalist. **Food is medicine.**

An athlete is a performer and a performer is an athlete. In the same way that an athlete knows their body and knows what makes them perform best, we, as performers, have exactly the same responsibility. Those in the elite circle have enormous self-knowledge.

Chapter Four: Exercises

Here is a selection of the aromatherapy, herbal and homeopathic remedies I used during my stage career. They worked for me. Each of us is very different and you need to experiment with what works for you. Get professional advice on anything you ingest. Try these out before you ever get on stage.

Aromatherapy
Take any of the aromatherapy essential oils and put a few drops in a good quality unscented body cream or lotion. In an instant, you have your own special formula at a fraction of the cost. Caswell Massey has great herbal body products. They have excellent quality and fabulous natural fragrances.

- **Lavender.** Quiets the nervous system and can help you fall asleep at night.
- **Cedar oil.** Clears the head.
- **A special treat** for a relaxing bath. To a deep tub of warm water, add four drops of **Vetiver**, six drops of **Sandalwood**, three of **Sage**, add a handful of **rose petals** sprinkled on the surface of the water. When you get out of soaking in this mixture, you will feel like new: even after a 30-hour journey. Guaranteed!
- **Peppermint oil.** I purchased a concentrated French formula in Paris and carried it with me. Whenever you have an upset stomach, a couple of drops of very intense peppermint in a small amount of clear water will help settle your stomach. Most health food stores have peppermint oil.

What are your remedies?

Homeopathic remedies

- **Rescue Remedy**. My favorite of all time is the Bach Flower, *Rescue Remedy*. I always kept it in my theater kit.
- **Tiger Balm**. Another important and essential all-purpose remedy is Tiger Balm. I bought it for the first time in Singapore. Tiger Balm is widely available in US drugstores. It has a smell reminiscent of American Vicks VapoRub, but better. If scenery or a crazed colleague runs into you, apply Tiger Balm. The bruise will dissipate by the next day and not turn black and blue! This saved me in the rough and tumble rape scene of *La Mancha*. It works. In addition, a touch of this powerful stuff on the outside of your nostrils will clear a stuffy head in an instant. It is also helpful to rub Tiger Balm on sore muscles, although you will smell like an apothecary's dream. Tiger Balm comes in two scents. The red is heavily clove scented, the white, less so. Don't apply Red Tiger Balm to your face, it's too powerful.
- **Ayr nasal gel** is the best yet! This gentle saline solution will cling to the inside of your nostrils and help prevent dryness on stage. It also helps filter out some of the suffocating stage dust.
- *Argentum nitricum*. Works for fear, anxiety and emotional upset.
- *Silica* or *Scilicea*. For low self-confidence.
- *Gelsemium*. Often prescribed for anxiety and helps with relief from diarrhea.
- *Ignatia*. Helps with emotional stress or the sensation of a lump in your throat.
- *Arnica (gel, cream, tablets)*. This works well for body aches and pains.

What are your remedies?

Herbal remedies

- ***Chamomile***. You can use the actual dried flowers and steep in a cup of boiling water for 5 to 10 min before drinking. There is also liquid extract chamomile available.
- ***Oatstraw*** (*Avena Satvia*). Soothes the nervous system and relieves stress. It is very gentle.
- ***Skullcap***. Relieves nervous tension and is available as a liquid extract or powder. I found skullcap too relaxing for performance.
- ***Kava Kava, Passiflora, Orange Flower*** and **Valerian**. Soothers. You can find these in a combination capsule in a health food store. They help with jet lag and soothe you to sleep rather than taking chemical sleeping aids.

What are your remedies?

Chapter Five
The People in the Dark

Audiences are the same all over the world, and if you entertain them, they'll respond.
                                                            - Liza Minnelli, singer & actress

Suppose *you* are the enemy, instead of your audience? Is it possible that you are projecting your fears onto people who only wish you well? At the end of a performance, is it tear-yourself-down-time?

Here you will learn techniques to make friends with your audience. You will learn how to assess your performance in a way that will serve you, instead of harm you.

Make friends with the enemy
Yes, there are hostile audiences occasionally but it's rare. For example, if an audience paid top dollar and was expecting Luciano Pavarotti, but at the last minute, he was replaced with tenor X from Lower Slobovia, they might feel some hostility.

In general, an audience wants you to succeed for two reasons. One, they paid good money for these tickets and two, they *want* to be transported somewhere else. They want to be carried off in the arms of art. That job is our privilege and our responsibility.

That statement alone lets you know it's about *them,* not us. We are here to reveal deeper truths and moments of creativity that are transformative. If we are immersed in self-criticism while we are performing we are depriving them, and ourselves, of the joy of creativity. The time for analysis is in the studio NOT on stage while you are performing.

Change your focus
I don't know who started it, but there is a traditional suggestion that you should imagine the audience in their underwear. I really have no interest in anyone's underwear. In some cases that would be most disturbing or just plain funny. Instead, let's look at some common sense ways of creating a comfort zone with your audience.

Do you stare, deer-in-the-headlights style, at your audience and break the fourth wall? That's the imaginary wall that encloses your scene on stage and separates you from your audience. Did you know you can change your visual focus so that everything beyond the edge of the stage is a blur?

I watched a 2005 interview with Diane Sawyer and <u>Barbra Streisand</u>. It was interesting that Barbra said that she couldn't possibly sing in anyone's living room because she could see everyone's eyes. The people would be right there on top of her. She had much less of a problem when there were huge lights shining in her eyes and there was a sea of 20,000 people out there in the dark. That scenario made her feel much more comfortable. Comfortable or not, Barbra didn't sing live on stage for 27 years because she went up (forgot the words) on three songs during her televised Central Park concert.

If you wear glasses for distance, you can do what Maria Callas did. Callas took off her glasses and the world beyond her stage set became a blur. Even the conductors were difficult for her to see. That wasn't a problem because she had worked with them so closely, they were breathing with each other.

You can practice this technique by holding your arm and hand out in front of you and gazing fixedly at your hand. You will realize as you focus only on that distance that everything beyond it becomes slightly out of focus. It's the same as manually focusing a camera lens on the foreground. You can develop that technique with practice so it is there for you when you need it.

Create a bubble
One of my favorite tools, and one that I have seen work with my clients and students, is to create a personal world. How would you feel if you could walk into an imaginary bubble and know that everything in that space was put there by you? It would be like putting a one-way mirror up on the fourth wall. Imagine yourself encased in a bubble that is like a one-way mirror. The audience can see in. You can't see out. You can put trees and an ocean in front of you. You can put people you love inside of that bubble. How about your grandma sitting in a chair with a loving smile on her face?

This method made a dramatic difference in the performance of a classical pianist who became so nervous that phrases and refinements he had labored over for months disappeared into thin air. In my master class I asked him what was his favorite place on earth. He told me it was the beach in Miami. We had a lot in common. I have the same love. Together we described a beautiful location on the beach with palm trees. The sunset was happening with gorgeous orange, pink, purple, blue and yellow painting the sky. The surf was gently lapping against the shore, broken only by the occasional screech of a seagull.

Into that setting, we placed an exquisite nine-foot grand that was magically immune to sand, to moisture, or to any of the things that would harm the piano. He was alone in this beautiful setting and totally at peace. When he began the first notes of the Rachmaninoff again, everything was different. There was an absolute focus and an outpouring of his inner self that was simply riveting. Everyone in the audience felt it.

Treat yourself and create your own magical setting. Set the stage as you would for the most comfortable, relaxing and gratifying experience you can imagine. Bring that setting on stage with you and enlarge it to encompass the entire stage. If you have a conductor, enlarge the bubble just enough to include the orchestra pit and the Maestro. Let the rest of the world just fade away. Try it. It's remarkable!

The magic of the present
Whether or not you create a bubble is up to you. However, it is vital for any performer to remain absolutely and totally in the moment. You can't be in two places at one time. I cannot tell you how many times I have seen a student performing and right beside that student I can see a curious little being. This make-believe gnome has three or four arms, one eye in the middle of its forehead, snaggly teeth and one long, pointed index finger on each hand. This imaginary creature, *Mr. NyetGoodEnuf*, stands there pointing at the performer muttering

aloud. "Oops, that wasn't the way you practiced it! Ouch, that was flat. Ach, do you really think that was a tone?"

Overall, Mr. NyetGoodEnuf thoroughly upstages the performer. He doesn't give a darn about art and doesn't care that he's taking all the focus. Take the focus back but take yourself lightly. Have fun with creating your bubble and annihilating this creature who upstages you. Benjamin Zander, conductor and speaker extraordinaire has a rule we need to put up in our practice space, "Don't take yourself so . . .damn seriously!"

Performance is not the place for self-criticism. Our Zen studio is the place to pay attention to every detail. The stage and performance is the place where we remove all the structure of our practice and polishing. It is the same as removing the scaffolding when a building is completed. Here we create a spontaneous work of art within the parameters we have defined and worked on.

Sharing vs. showing off

> *Creative work is play. It is free speculation using materials of one's chosen form.*
> - Stephen Nachmanovich, violinist & author

Remember my story of the child playing in the hot sun? The one who joyously offered you melting M&Ms? Of all the methods I have presented here, *the best way to soothe stage fright into control is to explain and share what you love with someone else.* In this case, that someone else is an audience. What you love is your art form.

Think of how patient, loving and excited you are when you are telling a story to a young child. Are you worried they will criticize your way of telling the story? No. You are sharing something that you love. My grandmother translated and shared stories of the operas as we listened to the Metropolitan Opera broadcasts when I was a little girl. Her love of the art form was so magnetic and so attractive I cried. I couldn't wait to become involved in this beautiful world. Her love, and her sharing of that love, is what intoxicated me.

Instead of, "Listen to how beautifully I can play this passage!" What would happen if you asked instead, "Do you realize what happens to your heart and your mood when you hear the change from C major to C minor?" Don't just perform something to show off your technique. *Share* your understanding of the music. *Share* the way it is expressed. *Share* and it will change the dynamic of fear completely. I promise you it will. Again, I say this will not happen overnight. Little by little you will find the exhilaration of sharing and your fear will be transformed into positive performance excitement. In *The Art of Possibility*, Benjamin Zander said it perfectly.

I tell my students, "Imagine you are [a] pianist and you meet someone who has no familiarity with – perhaps has never even heard –the E-minor prelude of Chopin. You might want to sit down next to him at the piano and say, 'Listen to the theme in the right hand. See how it holds together over the arch of four bars, and then the melody goes down one step? Listen to the constantly changing harmonies in the left hand, how they ring every possible change in the melody note... and so on.' As you get caught up in the excitement of explaining and sharing the music with your companion, would you have the time to be nervous? Of course not! It wouldn't occur to you. But this is exactly what you're doing when you perform – you are pointing to the beauty and the artistry of the music.[2]

Instead of pointing to yourself and asking, "Am I not magnificent?" Share your understanding, passion and mastery of an art form you love. BIG difference.

An unexpected perk of this sharing is intimacy. You are inviting your audience to share your experience. There's something very intimate about that. You are not just sharing the hours of refinement and rehearsal that you have put into your performance. That work is part of your job description and not their concern. You are sharing *why* you think this piece, this work, is so worthy of your love and attention. You want to explain that in a sincere and intimate way to the people who have come here to be carried away. You want them to share your wonderful discovery. If you find this path, you will become so engrossed in your telling of the story and so single-minded and focused, that ordinary things won't matter and your fear will lessen.

Personal experience
My refuge was going so deeply into the present moment I had no time to think about what anyone thought of me. I didn't want to be anywhere else than where I was at that moment. I was involved in what I was doing and I was doing it with 100% of my attention, passion and commitment. I didn't notice whether someone was picking his nose or texting his buddy.

So intent was I, that in a dress rehearsal as Carmen in Act I at Houston Grand Opera, I stamped out the cigarette I was smoking, as directed, and went on. The scene was going very well. I was amazed to see the director tearing down the center aisle of the brand new Wortham Theater. He stopped the scene and I wanted to know what the problem was.

He said, "You simply can't stamp out the cigarette that way."

I asked, "Why not? We have a ground cloth."

"Adria, you can't – the audience will be horrified. You just stamped it out with your bare foot!"

"Oh. . ." That is what I mean by concentration and I promise you, I felt absolutely nothing and there was no burn on the bottom of my foot. No, I don't have calluses.

Use the nervous energy
Have you watched a horse in the starting gate? Have you seen a runner prepare for a race? That anticipatory energy is magical. It provides the kind of fuel that very few situations can. If you have warmed up, if you know your music or presentation inside out, if you have rehearsed (good habits, not bad), you are on a fast track. If you feel well physically, if you're excited about the music, script or work you're performing and you can't wait to share it, you have a lead in the race.

The excited quivering of every nerve as you wait in the wings is a little bit scary, yes? But it is also exhilarating. Use that energy. Use that anxiety, as a battery to fuel your expression. That energy sets us apart as performers. That energy raises the ordinary to the extraordinary. Focus that energy stream to a receptive audience. They want to experience the magic. That is why they came to the theater in the first place.

If you make a mistake
Okay, you're on stage and everything is going beautifully. You're in the flow and suddenly you forget the words right in the middle of the scene and it throws you for a loop. What do you do? I say go on. One of the most important things you can do for yourself is to use improvisation in preparation for any performance. Give yourself worst-case scenarios and find immediate and practical ways to respond to the problematic situation.

Practice what would happen if a string breaks. Practice what would happen if you forget your lines. Do you know your scene well enough to be able to make up an approximation of a line? Have you built enough trust with your colleagues on stage to know they will be there for you if they hear deathly silence? In theatrical terms, eternity is truthfully defined as the time that passes between a dropped cue and the next line. Only rarely will a mistake be so horrendous that it brings everything to a screeching halt. That is when you turn to the audience, beg their indulgence, put a smile on your face and walk back into your bubble. This is *live* theater. It will happen.

A note on the vital importance of teamwork in theater: don't think because you are the star, you are alone in your solitary shining and don't need anyone. Thank your colleagues, the stagehands, the light man, the sound engineer, your costumers, and your team. Without them, you are a solitary, invisible, ordinary figure in a black box with no light. Get it? Good.

There is no substitute for kindness and consideration. Say 'please' and say 'thank you.' If you do, you will be remembered fondly. One of my prized possessions is a bath toy. It is a tiny yellow duck in a pharaoh's makeup and headdress. The props department at Utah Opera made it for me for *Aida*. Not only were they pros, but we were colleagues. I never forgot that. They even painted goldfish in my bath for my skinny dip in Act II. Oh, we had fun!

Prepare for the worst and prepare for the best: then, jump in the pool. This is why live theater is so exciting. It's a tight rope. You could fall off anytime.

Here's an important question: If it's all so horrible, what are you doing here? You can leave. No one is holding a gun to your head and making you perform. I think this is a key point. Ask yourself again: why am I performing? What is the payoff when it works well, or even when it doesn't? If you have decided to stay in the business, read on.

After the performance
In any business you have periodic performance reviews that contain specific information that helps an employee improve. So, what happens in the arts? I have heard performers walk off stage and immediately begin badmouthing themselves. "That was horrible, I was choking on phlegm, my embouchure was mush, my fingers were spastic..." I could go on for pages. Is that helpful? No. Criticism is a very valuable part of our work on stage and it's an excellent tool

for growth. However, *constructive criticism is criticism that adds value. It tells someone specifically what he or she needs to do to improve.*

How to criticize constructively

Criticism may not be agreeable, but it is necessary. It fulfills the same function as pain in the human body. It calls attention to an unhealthy state of things.
-Winston Churchill, statesman

When you're finished greeting your adoring public and sitting quietly at home drinking a cup of hot tea, start making a list. No, make that a list with four columns. In the first column, enter the performance date. Write the things that worked in your performance, the things that went well. In the third column, write the things that did not go well. In the fourth column, list possible solutions to the problem. You have an evaluation form in the exercises following this chapter.

Take this paper as soon as possible to your teacher or coach. You don't want to forget the details. Don't let weeks go by. Be an Olympic athlete. Dissect and correct until it is the very best you can make it. If your teacher was there the critique will be detailed and easily understood. If you're already a pro, take this to your coach and either bring a video or describe what happened.

If you are fortunate, you have a coach who knows the art of constructive criticism. Some do not, and they can be extremely cruel. Many performers have thin skins. That is not an asset. Your attitude is essential in helping you progress. If you feel all criticism is negative no matter how beautifully it's delivered and you feel your self-esteem growing less when you are being critiqued, you need to cure yourself of those qualities. It's part of being a professional. Learning from constructive criticism is part of mental toughness. On the other hand, some people who think they are giving you constructive criticism are not actually being helpful. They are tearing you down as a person, not criticizing an aspect of the performance. *Constructive criticism should be a reasonable, unemotional evaluation of a performance with the purpose of educating.*

If you *always* feel personally attacked, this is a good time for you to evaluate how much you have improved artistically with this coach or teacher versus how good they are at giving you excellent and supportive feedback. No one is perfect. Does the positive outweigh the negative? Sometimes an excellent coach doesn't work well with a client because of a personality conflict. Sometimes personal problems are in the way. Finding someone whom you respect, who asks a great deal from you and with whom you make progress, is essential. In the ZEBRA exercises, you will find a chart and questions to make your evaluation of your coach or teacher easier. *An important point to remember is that you hire the teacher, not the other way around.* If they are not working out for you, it's time to move on.

Let's say you have a teacher who insists you do vocal exercises that repeatedly make you hoarse. You try with all you heart to do what she wants and yet, you end up with damaged vocal cords. No matter, how difficult, it's time to leave. Singing must NEVER hurt.

Your thoughts and your criticism of yourself should be respectful and constructive. You need to be aware that criticism and revision are a continuing and ongoing process. *As long as you are performing, you will be refining.* You will never reach your musical and theatrical nirvana and stop working on your craft. If you do, move over and let someone else have the spotlight. That's why I insist you make two lists. A list of positives is as important as what went wrong with the performance. That's how you grow.

After performance questions

- What was the overall feeling of the performance?
- How was the pacing?
- Where did I get tired?
- How were my lyrics/dialogue, phrasing, dynamics, interpretation?
- Was I distracted or focused?
- I felt wonderful, what did I do in preparation for this performance?
- I felt horrible, what did I do in preparation for this performance?
- What specific moments or passages need more work?
- What moments or passages felt organic and true?
- How can I improve my work?

There is a chart in the exercises for you to answer these questions. Have you noticed that you often speak to yourself in a way that you would never speak to a colleague or to a friend? Be kind. Most of us are guilty of this. I have old voices in my head that are disparaging, "Gee, that was stupid. You're so dumb." I wouldn't dream of saying that to a student or to a client. Become mindful of that, and change it. More on that later.

To film or not to film
I don't think it is beneficial for beginning students to film themselves and obsessively watch that film again and again, picking out what they did wrong. Self-consciousness is not helpful. Self-*awareness* is what we're after. After a couple of years of performing experience, video becomes a very helpful thing. Even a professional is better off waiting before reviewing a taped performance unless they are doing so with their coach. Give yourself some space and time before you evaluate yourself.

Once you have some objective distance and can make both positive and negative commentary on the video and performance, it becomes an invaluable tool for your progress. You will be able to see that you are conducting with your right elbow. You're tapping your left foot, or the core of your body is closed in on itself, not allowing you freedom with the bow.

Be kind, be gentle to yourself, but be open-minded and willing to learn and evolve. Criticism about your technique is not a personal insult. Criticism about your dress and how you present yourself, is again, not personal.

If you want to learn and you want to excel, refinement of your natural talents and gifts is essential. You need a method of learning that will allow you to rehearse, refine, evaluate and perform in a way that controls anxiety and stage fright. You need a method that allows you to get on the path to peak performance.

Before we explore the ZEBRA method, do you realize you have a secret weapon? Well, maybe not so secret – but it is powerful. Do you remember when I said performance was a business? Do you realize you have business tools readily available?

Chapter Five: Summary

An audience wants you to succeed. **They paid good money for the tickets** and **they want to be carried away by a theatrical experience.**

Change your visual focus so that everything beyond the edge of the stage is a blur. It's like focusing a camera lens on the foreground. The objects in the background become blurry.

Create a bubble: Create a personal world and imagine yourself in a bubble that is a one-way mirror. **The audience can see in, you can't see out.** Put whatever and whomever you want in that bubble. Get comfortable.

You must remain absolutely and totally in the moment. If you stand outside of yourself criticizing, *Mr. NyetGoodEnuf*, your imaginary friend, is upstaging you. Banish him!

From Benjamin Zander: "**Don't take yourself so . . . damn seriously!**"

Sharing vs. showing off: Share what you love (your art) **with someone else** (the audience).

None of this will happen overnight.

Get into the present moment: If you are **intently focused on what you're doing right now,** you won't have time to think about what anyone else thinks of you.

If you make a mistake, go on.

Use improvisation to prepare for the best-case scenario and the worst-case scenario.

Teamwork is essential. Without your colleagues, stagehands, lighting, sound engineer, costumes, the marketing team - you are an invisible, ordinary figure in a black box with no light.

Make two lists: things that worked in your performance, things that did not go well and in a third column, a solution to the problem. There is a convenient chart in the exercises that follow.

Analyze the performance with your coach or teacher. Olympic athletes go over every detail of their performance, take it apart and make it better.

Constructive criticism adds value. Tell someone what he or she needs to do to improve. It's part of mental toughness; a reasonable, unemotional evaluation of the performance with the purpose of educating. **Criticism and revision are improvements that never end.**

Self-consciousness is not helpful: **self-awareness is.**

Chapter Five: Exercises

The exercises for this chapter are designed to give you practice with changing your focus, with building your bubble on stage, analyzing your performance constructively, getting into the present moment and becoming more comfortable and appreciative of the power of sharing.

Change your focus exercise.
Settle back into a comfortable chair and take three deep belly breaths. Let them out with a sigh. You can also listen to the *Cycle of Nine*, a breathing and relation exercise explored in Chapter 10. It puts you in the perfect frame of mind and state of relaxation for optimal performance.

Hold your hand out in front of you, rest it on a table, or object in front of you. Concentrate on remaining relaxed and staring fixedly at your hand in front of you. The object of this exercise is that as you stare at your hand and attempt to bring it more and more into focus, I want you to notice how the things around your hand and around your body become slightly fuzzy. They lose focus.

Don't do this for a long period of time. At first, start with a maximum of five minutes. The second and third time you do it, increase it to 10 minutes. Soon you will notice that when you choose, you can focus your eyes in such a way that whatever you have close to you (or in the foreground) becomes the object of your energy. Whatever else is beyond that goes into a fuzzy world that does not concern you. Focus and concentration are two of the keys that allow you to do your best on stage.

Once you become practiced and comfortable with this exercise, you'll be able to do it any time you wish. You can practice it throughout the day. Looking at an object and allow the objects around it to become fuzzy and out of focus. In a way, you are being a master photographer and focusing your attention on what you want your audience to experience.

For this, or any of the other exercises we do, a kitchen timer is a great tool for helping us budget our time. Rather than carry anything around, we can use our smart phones, or sport watch with a timer. Play with what works for you and begin to use your time more efficiently.

List anything here that makes this exercise more comfortable for you:

Present moment exercise

Only that day dawns, to which we are awake.
– Henry David Thoreau, American writer and philosopher

Wake up! Do you have any idea how much chatter we have going on in our minds and how many miraculous technologies compete for our attention? This exercise will help you focus your concentration, your level of contentment and your health. I'm not exaggerating a bit.

Settle back in your chair and get comfortable. Take and release three deep belly breaths or use the *Cycle of Nine* to get you in the proper state of relaxation.

Concentrate solely on your breathing. You monkey mind will drag in all sorts of thoughts for you to play with. Simply say *thinking, thinking,* and **come back to the present moment**. This sounds a lot easier than it is. Instead of getting annoyed with yourself, notice the thinking and come back to the breathing.

Once you **master two or three minutes of mental stillness,** you will begin to notice a change in the clarity of your thought processes and new personal magnetism.

Now let's take this a step beyond. Once you are quiet and still, focus on your breathing with your eyes closed. Now begin to **notice the sounds, the smells and the sensations around you**. How well can you identify everything around you? When you do this in a familiar space, you should be able to slip into the gap between your thoughts quite easily. When you're in an unfamiliar space you will have more difficulty but your senses will awaken in a new way.

When you open your eyes, you will have a new appreciation of the world around you. Just because you can't see something doesn't mean it's not there. **Take that newfound stillness and carry it like precious cargo on stage with you.** If you communicate from that stillness, your audience and you will connect far more easily.

What things, sounds and smells do you notice in your present moment?

Chart for after performance questions. Make copies and use these guidelines for constructive criticism. Use in conjunction with the performance critique charts.

What was the overall feeling of the performance?	
How was the pacing?	
Where did I get tired?	
How were my lyrics/dialog/phrasing/dynamics/interpretation?	
Was I distracted or focused?	
I felt great. What did I do to prepare for this performance?	
I felt horrible. What did I do to prepare for this performance?	
What specific passages or moments needed more work?	
What moments or passages felt organic and true?	
How can I improve my work?	

Create your bubble exercise

Remember our discussion about creating a bubble onstage that you would fill with the people, places and things you loved? Now it is your turn to actually populate your bubble.

What would make you comfortable?

Who would make you comfortable?

Are you alone?

Where are you?

What time of day is it?

What is the temperature like?

What are you wearing?

Armed with magnetic stillness and your newly sharpened focus, let's create the bubble. Let's create a comfort zone designed by you and for you. You are the set designer. On this set, put in the things, objects and people that make you comfortable.

Draw, cut out pictures, or put in words to give you an idea of the reality you will create. Design your ideal setting. In your mental Zen studio, you can carry it with you anywhere!

Add your own details. Be specific. The more specific you are the easier it will be to call up your imaginary world onstage whenever you need it.

My stage bubble is set in a place I love, the beach in Miami early in the morning. The people who inspire me are there. My beloved grandmother smiles at me. My cats lounge around. My set has sand, plants, palm trees - it is my comfort zone. What is in yours?

What and who is in your bubble?

Your bubble

The sharing exercise

The purpose of this exercise is to find the key to your joy and your fearlessness. **How to do it: you are going to give away five things or five moments in 14 days.**

Choose something you feel comfortable giving. It must mean something to you now. You can't give away your horrible old shoes you were going to throw out anyway. That doesn't count.

On the right side of the sample list below, list things or moments you might share. Giving is giving, no matter whether we are giving a performance, a thing, or a precious bit of our attention.

After the first 14 days, you will get more comfortable. *I dare you to do this once a week for the rest of your life.* It will change far more than your outlook: it will change your life. I guarantee it.

What is your starting date? _____

Before you go to the next page and look at my suggestions, what ideas pop up for you? Write as fast as you can.

Sharing exercise

Take a young one who adores you to lunch or make a meal for a shut-in.	
Giveaway a new pair of shoes, or clothes that are not perfect for you.	
Forgive someone. Not forgiving is like drinking poison and expecting *them* to die.	
Give away your song/ dance/ music/ words to sick people or children in the hospital.	
Be truly present with someone (not on your phone) for at least 30 minutes. *Really listen*.	
Give your worn-out car to Kars for Kids, or donate 10% to a cause that matters to you	
Smile at a three strangers today.	
Send a sincere thank you note to someone who has helped you.	
Send a positive note to someone who hasn't done a darn thing for you, anonymously.	
Share your fears, they will lessen.	
Buy a small gift for someone for no reason at all.	
Teach someone they are enough. You will be surprised what you learn about yourself.	
Share your real feelings with someone, even if they are painful. Trust yourself.	

Questions to ask yourself about your coach

You're going to coach and spending time and money to get better at this skill you enjoy. If you knew better than they did, you would be the teacher. On the other hand, sometimes no matter how much skill your coach or teacher has, they may not be able to communicate it to you. It may be that you don't understand or mesh with their style of teaching.

The questions that I list here are only a partial list and of course subjective. The realm I inhabited was singing, theater and acting. I don't know the right questions for a violinist or a saxophonist having never attempted to play those instruments. So, make a list of questions that are unique your performance arena.

Two more important things: one, you are hiring the teacher, not the other way around. Two, no relationship is perfect. Getting along with a prickly pear who has a great deal to give you technically helps you learn a valuable skill in dealing with the difficult people you'll encounter in your life. *Your teacher does not have to be your best friend.* If that happens, you are very fortunate. They are holding a lantern up to illuminate the dark places on your path and make you a better performer.

Some possible questions. Circle yes or no. (I am using teacher and coach interchangeably here)

- Am I making progress with this teacher? Yes No
- Is this teacher asking me to do things that are painful? (For example, do I leave every lesson hoarse?) Yes No
- Are they abusive in any way? Yes No
- Do this teacher and I understand each other when they explain technique? Yes No
- Have I given this a wholehearted try? Yes No
- Does this coach inspire me? Yes No
- Does this teacher value my time as I value theirs? Yes No
- Does this coach give me constructive criticism? Criticism I can understand and use to change and raise my level of performance. Yes No
- In spite of how good this teacher is, do we have a major personality conflict that is in the way of my learning? Yes No
- One more time – am I making progress with this teacher? Yes No

Your questions

PERFORMANCE CRITIQUE

DATE & PLACE	GOOD	BAD	SOLUTION
University recital May 17	-- French group was great -- Looked good -- American group was super	-- German was a mess - Shoes were not comfortable - I was so nervous	- Did not work on the German as much because it was easy for me! Ironic -- Buy shoes with lower heels -- Worked so hard on the Am. contemporary pieces they became easy and the best of the night. Duh! -- Another dress rehearsal might have helped
Charity Concert Aug 15	- Had fun! - Perfect dress and sexy, comfortable shoes (didn't know that was possible!) -- The duets were good	- Forgot the words in the *Fair Lady* song, recovered well	- Write out the words a couple of more times - Must send thank you note to organizer. I want to do more of these. I gave out over 20 cards. Good for me. --Gotta finish web site asap!!

INSTRUCTIONS: Using this chart and the Performance Level Chart together will allow you to see a visual representation of your improvement over a period of time.

PERFORMANCE CRITIQUE

DATE & PLACE	GOOD	BAD	SOLUTION

INSTRUCTIONS: MAKE COPIES AS NEEDED. YOU CAN USE A WHOLE SHEET OR MORE FOR ONE PERFORMANCE. USING THIS PERFORMANCE CRITIQUE SHEET WITH THE PERFORMANCE LEVEL CHART WILL GIVE YOU A GREAT RECORD OF YOUR PROGRESS.

Chapter 6
Your Not So Secret Weapon

I have an almost religious zeal – not for technology per se, but for the Internet, which is for me, the nervous system of Mother Earth, which I see as a living creature, linking up.
- Dan Millman, gymnast, author

Do you realize that as a present-day artist you have a world of research, marketing and self-promotion available at your fingertips 24/7? Are you utilizing the variety of tools you have available to better study your performance and rehearsal practices? Are you aware of how visible you are to the world, for better or for worse? You have more control than you think.

If you are not using the incredible tools available to you, and you think that marketing and business are beneath your artistic sensibilities, you need to open your eyes. Are you afraid of technology? I'm not going to tell you stories about slogging through waist deep snow for miles to a one-room schoolhouse. I was raised in Florida. I *am* going to tell you stories about big, bulky reel-to-reel tape recorders, no Internet, no social media, no smart phones, and $1500 phone bills just to keep in touch with family, friends and lovers.

The tools available to you as an artist in today's world are a tremendous asset to your career. I want this brief chapter to illuminate the huge advantage you have over artists of the past. The internet, instantaneous communication, and connectivity are second nature to you. But sometimes what is normal loses its importance because it's so natural and easy. Let's not take the tools you have at your disposal for granted. Let's explore some of these tools and what they offer.

Warning: the world of technology is moving so fast that by the time this book comes out, the suggestions I make will already be obsolete and better options available.

The audiovisual world
When I was a teenager back in the dark ages, I was thrilled to be given a huge, heavy reel-to-reel tape recorder. I could record some of my vocal performances and playback others recorded in concert. It was too big and heavy to lug around, but it was an invaluable way to improve my performance skills. I was part of the technological elite to have such a wonderful machine. I was also one of the first in line to buy a Sony Pro tape recorder.

Now you have audio and video recorders to capture your performances and a record of your progress. You can share your performance work almost instantly with other artists or with family and friends; even with the entire world if you so desire. Beware: that could be a problem. Think like a marketer. Do not put anything - and I do mean *anything* – on the web you are not proud of. Use the private video option on YouTube if you want to share something with a select audience. I recently bought a highly rated portable recording device for under $400. It is smaller than two decks of playing cards. Isn't that extraordinary? The sound recording is of such a high level, it's actually suitable for voiceover work. My old tape recorder cost over $1,000. The first "portable" video cameras were so big they needed to be supported on your shoulder.

You couldn't record your latest performance the way you can now. Respect the orchestral clauses and laws about recording. Recording your own material is fine. When you add music composed by others, or other people are on the scene, you may have a problem with copyright infringement. Be aware and always get clearance.

Once you are no longer a beginning performer, a video camera can be one of your most valuable and inexpensive teachers. Make a list of what is positive about your performance and what is negative and needs to improve: its an excellent tool for self-discovery and growth.

The internet
Research and development for the internet was running full speed ahead in 1989 and the first website premiered in 1991. I didn't jump on board until 1995 when running my life was almost impossible because I was on the road from 6 to 10 months a year. At the time, I wasn't making enough money to hire a full-time personal assistant. I needed to pay bills and communicate easily and efficiently throughout the world with my agents, concert promoters and directors.

Most of you reading this book have grown-up with the internet as part of your everyday life. I want to stress the impact professional use of the web has on your business. Yes, your career is a business. The web has extended your reach from the interpersonal to the global.

E-mail and communication
Please do yourself and everyone else a favor and get a professional email address. Poopsiedoopsie@aol.com does not cut it in the professional world. Neither does Niftylownotes, etc. Use your name. Be professional. If you are Ariel Smith, make your email a.smith@gmail.com or arielsmith@asmith.com.

The way you communicate says a lot about you. Does your phone blare tinny sounding music? The latest songs are great but remember to put your phone on vibrate in a meeting. Give precedence to the live people in front of you, not to a ringing phone. Technology is *your* servant, not the other way around.

In my career, I spent thousands of dollars in long distance telephone calls and faxes every month. Life goes on, no matter where we are or what we are doing. I was a glamorous road warrior, but I still wanted to talk to my friends. I also needed to take care of family problems. Once I even had a house closing with faxes flying from the US to Hong Kong. It cost me a lot of money. Long distance relationships are so much easier now because you can actually see each other when you talk with Skype or any other VoIP. At the time, I handled most of my business communication via fax. Now e-mail and scanning makes it all so much easier and more convenient. Use it wisely. Be aware of hitting reply to all - unless you really mean to!

You are your own press agent
You have a word processor and can create professional looking documents at the drop of a hat. You have spell check. Remember though, spell check doesn't know the difference between too, to or two. You can create a flyer for a free concert you're offering to the public.

You can write a press release and put it on your business Facebook page. You can create professional quality materials with just a little bit of attention and care.

If you can't afford a publicist yet, you even have a solution for that. I feel you don't need the expense of a publicist until you are on sure footing professionally and are being hired on a regular basis. However, publicity and marketing are absolutely essential for your professional success. Remember your career is a business. You might have the most magnificent voice, be the most incredible cellist, be the Baryshnikov of dance but if no one knows about you, no one can hire you. First step: create a website.

Your website

> *Looking at the proliferation of personal web pages on the Net, it looks like very soon everyone on Earth will have 15 megabytes of fame.*
> *- M.G. Sriram, professor of symbolic systems biology*

Your website is your worldwide calling card: it needs to be quality.

Your image is out there for the whole world to see. Make sure that is congruent: that it matches who you are as a person and as a performer. Be honest about your performances. Be honest about your experience. Exaggerations and overstatements are going to reveal themselves eventually. People tend to believe what they read so be careful of what you say. Because of the ability to research background information almost instantaneously, future employers can find out what is true and what is not.

Do your research and find out what looks good and works best on the web. If you don't have the ability to set up your own website, do the research and find guidelines to follow. Take a class: it will serve you well in the future. If you have the funds, hire an expert. Barter your services for a web presence. For example, offer to play at someone's wedding or at a party. In exchange have that person, who has web expertise, build a website for you.

For the singers among you, the magazine *Classical Singer* offers a webpage format that is simple and reasonably priced. Get a domain name (the simpler and easier to spell the better) and set up a free website on sites such as Google, Doteasy or GoDaddy. They are so many sites with free web hosting and free web site builders, which make it easier and faster. Unless you are doing e-commerce, a few simple, informative pages are all you need to get started.

Answers your website must provide

- Who are you? Think about who you are without the label of your work. We need to get a glimpse of the real you on a website.
- What is your talent? What is the product you are selling?
- Add a CURRENT professional photo. You do yourself a grave disservice when you put a picture on a website or program from 20 years, or 40 pounds, ago. This is a visual world. We need to know what you look like today. Make sure it's flattering and it looks like you.

- If you have a superlative review, make sure the four items just mentioned and the great review is above the fold on your webpage. What do I mean by above the fold? Picture a folded newspaper. The most important stories and headlines are always on the first page, above the fold, to catch the readers' eye. You want to do the same thing with your essential information.
- If you have an excellent recording or video of your work make sure that too, is available on the first page. If it's not excellent, don't use it. What I mean by excellent is that it *accurately shows what you can do at this point in your professional life.*
- List your performance experience. In the professional world, no one is interested what you may do in the future. They want to know what you are ready to do right now.
- Then list additional reviews, experience or photos.
- Make your contact page clear and easy. Pay attention to the professionalism I spoke about above when you choose your e-mail address.

I recommend a few wonderful books for website creation. Krug's, *Don't Make Me Think! A Common Sense Approach to Web Usability* is a great one. The books are available on my http://www.afiartists.com with a simple click.

Research saves you time and money
When I needed information on a role I was working on, I trudged across the river into New York City and sat for hours at the Lincoln Center Performing Arts Library. Now you can trudge across the room to your computer and all the information you need is at your fingertips.

You can find authentic pronunciation for foreign languages. You can find books, scores and music at enormous discounts from various websites. You can go to www.Gutenberg.org and find out-of-print books free. You can find the translation for art songs and arias. You can find musical and performance history with ease. You can hear and see the greatest in any field!

That easy research can save you lots of money. I spent 35 to 45% of my income on professional expenses. Want to increase your ROI (return on investment)? You can book your own flights and hotels and use sites that compare prices so you know you are getting the best deal.

Think of the time you'll save. Think of how much more time you will have to work on your craft. Or are you wasting time on Facebook all day? That question leads us to another asset or liability of the web: it depends on how you use it.

Research your future employers
If you are auditioning for concert master with a leading orchestra, do you think it would be helpful to know how the conductor feels about tempi or his conducting style? You bet. Does he bemoan the sloppiness of young performers? If so, shine your shoes, dress well (do that anyway). If you are auditioning for an opera director whose last three productions featured physically fit acting singers, step up time at the gym (do that anyway). In an interview with

Mr. X you read he hates the park n' bark singer. Plan your audition material accordingly. If an artistic director has just been interviewed and she declares her passion for Mahler, is that a clue for you? Of course it is.

When composer Giancarlo Menotti flew me to Rome to audition for his new production of *Carmen*, I dressed the part. The famed Spanish filmmaker, Carlos Saura was directing and RAI was filming it for European TV. I wore a dress with a skirt that moved. I wore my dance shoes and my castanets were tucked into my bra. I dressed for what my client wanted. Maestro Carigniani, the conductor, wrote in a fax to my agent in Spain, "It's not so much that she is an excellent Carmen, it is that she is the *only* Carmen in the world today."

Research will save you time, heartache and money. More important, it will focus your energies. I am not saying ignore your integrity and sell your soul. I *am* saying research your market, determine what is selling now and build your version of that. As a business (remember you are running a business) *you need to supply what your clients want, not what you think they need.* It's not fair or equitable, it simply – is.

Social media, pros and cons
Once again, I stress performing is a business like any other even though the soundtrack is better. Many people I know spend hours a day talking on Facebook or chatting with their friends. I assure you, that's not going to get you anywhere in the professional world.

Facebook offers exposure, as does MySpace, Twitter and all of the other emerging social media. Exposure can be a very good thing or a very bad thing. I'm sure you've read many times how in the business world, drunken pictures taken at a class reunion come back to haunt someone. What color you paint your nails, your growing embryo, your newest love, or your new car is not of interest to anyone except friends (or a crook). Be professional.

I once had a love whom I remember very distinctly not the least for something he said to me. I had written to him how much I cared. He turned to me very solemnly (he was a lawyer), and said, "Don't ever write anything down you don't want read in court." I have never forgotten those words. You would do well to remember them. Be aware your privacy is in your hands.

The advantages of social media are extraordinary. By creating a professional and personal network, you are building a brand for yourself. You are also building a network of people who can help you in your business ventures. Social media used in the right way can form a symbiotic network of people helping people. The professionalism and helpfulness of LinkedIn is extraordinary when used as a business tool, not social fluff.

You might be able to share a ride to the airport with a social media friend. You might be able to find an apartment in New York City or Hong Kong. Hotels are expensive. You can initiate the question and then contact the person privately. You don't want to announce to the world, "Y'all can come on in and pick up my big-screen, my brand-new Mac laptop and my 10 speed mountain bike."

None of these incredible tools was available to artists less than two decades ago. I want you to become proficient and responsible in using the web. Your smart phone, your computer and your interconnectivity with the world are powerful tools. If you use these tools with consistent professionalism, your pathway to the business fast lane is far more direct than it ever has been before. With power and control comes responsibility. The internet is a powerful tool: use it wisely. It is no longer a choice. You need to be first in line to respond to the latest information. Use it to your advantage.

Chapter 6: Summary

You have a world of **research, marketing and self-promotion available** at your fingertips 24/7.

Marketing is essential to your professional success.

Don't take the internet, instantaneous communication, and conductivity for granted. Use it well.

Use your audiovisual tools to aid you in constructive criticism of your performances. They do not replace a coach or teacher but they are an excellent reality check.

Get a professional e-mail address. Preferably, use Gmail or yourname@yourname.com. Don't be cute. Be professional.

Be considerate with your telephone usage. **Technology is your servant, not the other way around.**

Take responsibility for the fact that **you are your own press agent and you have the tools to be a good one.**

Your website is your global calling card.

Your website needs to provide:
- Who are you?
- What is your talent/product?
- What do you look like NOW?
- Reviews of your work.
- Excellent recordings or video.
- Your performance experience.
- A professional clear, easy contact page.

Research saves you time and money. Learn how to do it rapidly and well.

Don't waste time on social media. Use Facebook, MySpace, Twitter and all of the other emerging social media for positive and professional exposure.

Don't ever write anything down you don't want read in court.

You are responsible for your safety and privacy.

The Internet is a powerful tool. Use it wisely.

Chapter 6: Exercises

Your web page

Violet Valery, lyric soprano (who are you? & your talent/product)

Hear Ms. Valery Meow!

(Your current photo)

Mrs. Valery's interpretation was astoundingly beautiful. Her meowing filled the hall with beauty. Her acting skills need development, but they are on firm and steady paws.
- *New York Meow*

(Above the fold)

You've taken care of above the fold. Make sure your colors are pleasing on the computer screen and reflect who you are. Above all, your website needs to be clear and attractive.

In this part of the page you can add a picture and a review of your latest role, your performance experience and additional reviews.

Make sure you have an extremely clear contact page. People need to be able to reach you. *Your name.com* gives you a very professional e-mail address and you can link all of your e-mails to come into one central mailbox.

What I'm telling you is, of course, skeletal knowledge. You may be an internet maven already. I just want to give you a basic idea. There are many valuable books out there.

Check out the successful performers you admire and go to their websites. If you see something you like, model your site in a similar way. However, if you see a site with a picture that no longer looks like the performer, the background and sound effects of NASCARs (even though you love racing) and a wild and illegible font, don't copy it. Keep looking!

Your business card
In designing a business card, make sure you deliver your contact information and perhaps a picture. Realtors always put their picture on a card, so their clients get comfortable with

them. Although most performers don't do this, if it appeals to you, it might be worth a try. It certainly helps when the person you given the card to remembers your face but not necessarily your name. Here on your card, they can tie the two together.

Vistaprint.com is one of the many places you can get very reasonably priced business cards. Be aware that 250 free cards are *almost* free. You have to pay for anything except a blank back of the card. You pay for a glossy finish and you pay for shipping. Order normal standard shipping. It will usually arrive in a reasonable time frame unless you are in a rush.

Have your business card and your website coordinate with each other. Remember, you're aiming for a package, a brand that reflects you. Good business, right?

Put that same business card at the end of every e-mail you send out. Make sure it has a live link to your webpage. Again, we're aiming for a consistent look all across the board. This way you're much easier to remember.

Three rules for business cards: clarity, clarity, clarity. Play with some designs:

What's in your studio?
What are the tools for a basic comfortable studio that allows you to work comfortably and well?

First, if you are fortunate enough to have a personal space (even if it's your bedroom for now) take the time to invest your energy and work into transforming the space into a comfortable one. Give it a **coat of paint** and **storage**. Install inexpensive shelves to hold your music. Pick up a used filing cabinet. Check out thrift stores and Habitat for Humanity if you want to purchase inexpensive building materials.

Have a **music stand, a full-length mirror** and a **comfortable place to sit** when you're working on lines and memorization. Have a hand mirror too so you can check a 360 degree of yourself. Design a **do not disturb sign** and stick to it when you hang it on the door.

This is your time. You've earned it. Quality practice time is the very least of what your art deserves.

Invest in a **video camera** that will allow you to hear and see your performances as well as your practice sessions. Pay attention to your body language. Watch a lesson with your coach. Always ask permission when you're taping or recording anyone. Do not put it on YouTube unless you get a release. You can get sued if you don't.

Get a good quality recorder, I have one or two listed in resources on www.afiartists.com. **Audio recording** allows you to hear whether all the color you've invested in your sound is actually audible. Or does someone only get it when they see you and hear you? Does your clarinet melisma wail of sadness, or is it just a cold, technical decoration?

A tip for buying just about anything: don't spend money on the very latest release. Purchase a model that is a year old with the bugs already worked out. You'll get more bang for your buck.

What's on your wish list?

Your handle
Do you like your name? Really like your name? Do you realize if you don't like it you can change it? A name is a very powerful thing. Think about it. It is what you are called in this world.

Think of the actor John Wayne. He was born Marion Robert Morrison. Do you think that name would have turned him into The Duke or what if they named him Herby? Marilyn Monroe was born Norma Jean Baker. I rest my case.

Experiment with numerology when trying on names. It's absolute fun. Numerology is the science of numbers and names. The date you were born and the letters of your name all have numeric values. Those values help explain who you are and are a sort of map of your life. It's a fascinating field. Try it. If you are interested, there are a couple of good books on the subject I suggest on the website.

Space for names

PART TWO

THE ZEBRA METHOD

By three methods we may learn wisdom.
First, by reflection, which is noblest.
Second, by imitation, which is easiest.
And the third by experience, which is the bitterest.
— *Confucius*

Chapter 7
Z is for Your Zen Studio

I've discovered that numerous peak performers use the skill of mental rehearsal and visualization. They mentally run through important events before they happen.
- Charles A. Garfield, peak performance expert

Are you ready to create a space where stage fright is harnessed, focused and used as performance fuel? It isn't a pill. It's a path. Would you like to get better use out of your practice time? You can change your performance experience. Using deliberate practice and visualization, you can move from fuzzy to focus and from fear into peak performance.

I would love to be able to say that I guarantee if you follow this method to the letter, you will be free of all anxiety and every performance will be a work of art. Nothing, and no one, can guarantee you that. Live performance is too risky. The kind of stage fright that paralyzes you as a performing artist may not be the same as that of a colleague.

Follow a method, or methods, that work well for you. But remember that even when you are in the midst of a very successful career, you can have the same nervousness that affected cellist Pablo Casals even into his 90s. He went on to play in spite of his discomfort. So is the definition of courage not to be free of fear, but to walk on in spite of it? I know it is!

Throughout my career, nervousness and stage fright have never left me before playing. And each of the thousands of concerts I have played at, I feel as bad as I did the very first time.
- <u>Pablo Casals</u>, Spanish cellist and conductor

The ZEBRA structure

I would visualize things coming to me. It would just make me feel better. Visualization works if you work hard. That's the thing. You can't just visualize and go eat a sandwich.
- Jim Carrey, actor

The ZEBRA method is designed as a framework for nurturing optimum performance. It will help you control anxiety and eliminate negative self-talk. It is a method of deliberate practice and efficient, relaxed preparation. It utilizes breath and visualization. This is your space for calm, productive work.

As performers, we need a private place for work: a place where we can take out a magnifying glass and examine every note, every word, and every facet of our art. This must be a serene, nurturing environment. We need a mental refuge. We need a space where we are free to create and free from criticizing, prying eyes. This is not only a physical space; it's a creative mental space as well. This is an area where you experiment. It's a place to make whopping mistakes and laugh at yourself, to fall down and get up again. This is a space where you are as demanding as you need to be, but never abusive.

The mental space

A great deal of importance and time rests on the physical preparation for performance. An equally important priority is your mental preparation. In time, you will find the skills, techniques and rituals that help you develop optimum performance.

The ZEBRA method, has nothing to do with religious practice, but draws on Zen practice for focus and relaxation. The practice of Zen involves a state of nothingness: a state of focus that unites body and mind. In our mental Zen studio, we are learning to be more focused, mindful and self-aware.

Visualization is a key component of your Zen studio. When you have decided what works for your pre-performance planning, you need to be able to visualize your routine with intense clarity.

All people visualize, because visualizing is part of the brain's daily business. But many people are not in the habit of paying attention to these images. They don't know they are being influenced by them. . . .That's one of the advantages of visualizing; it helps you gain objectivity in your life.[1]

Your visualization will help you attain control over your performance level and your nerves. Control is part of mental toughness. Ask yourself:

How do I want it to go? Then see it and feel it going that way and memorize that feeling by playing back that picture over and over. Your brain gets the message and plays it back to you when you need it. I assure you, that's how people succeed. It's not enough to know the theory about how visualizing works – you must practice and develop it as a skill so you have it when you need it. Replay in your mind your successful events and erase your failures.[2]

Once you have that self-awareness, you will develop a unique and very personal performance plan. That plan becomes the format into which you place your personal formula for success. You need to allow yourself the time to formulate the plan. Absorb it, try it out, and eliminate what doesn't work.

- **Your plan is yours alone** and not for anyone else's approval or comfort.
- Be present in your level of skill, experience and technique. **Don't be ahead of where you are right now.**
- **Take notes**. Pay attention to **your breakthroughs.** You'll begin to see a pattern as to what works and what doesn't.
- **Use it or lose it.** It's not just a saying. It's true. Practice the method you create with the same attentiveness that you practice your vocal, dance, acting or instrumental skills.
- **Practice the mental skills**. Mental toughness and mental skills are every bit as, if not more, important than our talent or our technique.

The physical space
If you are fortunate, you have a familiar rehearsal space where you practice your craft. Maybe it's a room at your University. Maybe a tiny sound studio you found that no one uses during a particular time of day. It may be your bedroom equipped with a keyboard and a mirror. You may use the studio where you rehearse with your coach or teacher or it may be a rented space. Wherever it is, it needs to be secure, comfortable and have complete privacy. Why? Because if a performer thinks someone is listening or watching, it becomes performance and not private rehearsal. It becomes a "reality show" which is absolutely real - except for the plot, the make-up, the lights, the director – you get my point, yes?

This is a physical space where you can talk to yourself in peace. Here you can establish rituals for performance that give you comfort and security. It is the place where you have the necessary instruments and equipment for your rehearsal sessions.

Budget time & energy
You will find you have more time than you think you do. More important than the length of time you have, is *how* you use that time. Learn your body rhythms. Are you more awake in the morning? Do you learn better in the afternoon or evening? Plan your work sessions for the hours when you're most alert and able to learn.

If you're at work or in school at your most productive time, take a break before you start working on your craft. Clear your mind with meditation or listening to music or doing yoga. Do not ignore transportation time: use it to practice. When you develop focus and concentration, you can get so much more work done.

Plan ahead for your week; allow time for your mental preparation. Get centered in your Zen studio before you begin your physical practice. It's a habit worth developing. Ten minutes of concentrated mental focus will give you enormous rewards. It is far more productive than 30 minutes of careless rehearsal.

Learn the skill first
Be patient with yourself. Remember, you have to learn these mental skills first before you can practice them. Mental skills don't take the same length of practice that physical skills do, *but they are more difficult to unlearn.* They are portable, so you can practice them anywhere. Your Zen studio is completely portable. In the section following this chapter, there are mental exercises and skills to practice when you are have time off or on public transportation. They will increase your invaluable skill of visualization. Just don't miss your stop!

None of this is a quick fix. Once you learn your rhythm for your best practice, you will know the time you need to prepare for a performance, an audition, or a recital. Just as important is personal time off.

Time off

You know how important a rest is in music, or the silences in a play? They are as important as the sound. You need time off too. Make sure you put that in the schedule as well. You need recreation, otherwise known as re – creation. According to popular lore, even the Lord rested. Plan for it.

What am I aiming for?

- You will work towards **consistency in performance**. Remember the difference between a professional and an amateur?
- You will work on the means to **focus your mental and physical rehearsal** in a way that gives you the most results for the time invested.
- You are aiming to **attain a degree of refinement** that places you on a professional level.
- You are aiming to achieve **a level of minimum skill** and a standard below which you do not fall.

Learn how to learn

My method is different. I do not rush into actual work. When I get a new idea, I start at once building it up in my imagination, and make improvements and operate the device in my mind. When I have gone so far as to embody everything in my invention, every possible improvement I can think of, and when I see no fault anywhere, I put into concrete form the final product of my brain.

- Nikola Tesla, pioneer of modern electrical engineering

When you are first learning your music, lines, choreography, you must have a plan. This plan utilizes the methods and skills that *work best for you* and makes the material and the technique a part of you. Here again, I caution you to accept your present level of skill and experience. Don't torment yourself by trying to be ahead of where you are.

Before the performance

You need a method that includes a mental and physical warm-up. Your mental warm-up includes how you speak to yourself and how confident you are in the strengths and qualities you have identified and acquired. Here you replace the habitual negative script with the positive one you have created.

Your physical warm up includes your stretches and exercises. Do you need to run 5 miles on the day you perform? Are you someone who needs to do an hour of stretching and an hour of meditation? This physical routine also includes your rest, your food and your dress. Then there is the warm up for your instrument.

Practice your mental and physical rituals to achieve a level of energy that is appropriate for you. This allows you to do your best: not what's best for someone else, but purely and uniquely for you.

Personal experience
As a leading lady, I had a lot of responsibility on my shoulders and it took an entire day to get ready for an opera. I have added a sample of my schedule in exercises. Create your own. We are all different and there is no right or wrong way to prepare. There is only the best way for *you* to prepare. For example, when I was doing eight shows a week as Aldonza in *Man of La Mancha*, I didn't have such an elaborate ritual. I slept as long as I could, did my yoga, minimal vocal warm-ups and ate well. That's all the time I had.

You have worked on your technique. You're confident you are at the best level you can be at this present time. You know what your strengths are. You know where your difficult spots are and have prepared for them. You know you are ready, and finally, you are looking forward to sharing with your audience. Before you leap into performance, have you looked at what worked for you in the past?

Review the past
Take stock of your successful performances and be honest with yourself. What worked and what did not? The next question is: *Why*? Write down how you prepared for those performances. Create separate areas such as mental, physical, technical and emotional preparation.

There are charts in the exercises that will make your task easier. Copy the blank forms and fill them out as needed. Keep a performance review log. You'll be able to see your progress. Make a note of your thoughts, your feelings, and your actions before these successful performances. Base your new plan on those things that have worked for you in the past. Throw the rest out. Each performance is a new beginning.

The performance
Here again, what works for *you* is of primary importance. It's true that we cannot control a great many things in our lives. Being as prepared as you can, for the best and the worst is good practice. It raises your odds for having a fine performance.

Remember that *professionalism means consistency*. It means performing on a level below which you do not fall. When you're lucky, you rise above that level and soar to new heights.

Having a plan allows you to focus on the essentials during the performance, and serves as banks to the river of your energy. Your energy needs focus to have power and to execute what you have envisioned. Sit down in your Zen studio and make a list as to what you need to do in the week or two before your performance.

- Where is the performance or audition and how do I get there?
- What will I wear?
- What, and when, do I need to eat on that day?
- How long do I need to sleep?
- What is the mental prep I need?
- Plan at least one, perhaps two dress rehearsals. No stopping even if the roof falls in.

The lists

On every single flight we (the crew) use checklists. Why? Lists prevent forgetting required steps during critical situations, for conformity of companywide operations and because some operations (emergencies for example) have too many steps to rely on memory alone for complete accuracy. The steps were put together after much study of what works best in light of past mistakes and thus ensures the safest and surest method of successfully resolving the problem.

- Lt. Col. John N. Mastroianni, Air Force & Civilian pilot, 39 years' experience

Experienced pilots have lists that they use with every flight. No matter whether I had an audition, rehearsal or performance, I always had a list that allowed me to relax about the basics. It's good practice. I had lists for packing, dressing, or for the routine I needed to do my best. It was all worked out. I learned what worked best for me and I had the forms in my computer. All I had to do was fill in the blanks and print. I've done the same for you. Adjust them to your needs.

How many lists do you need? Do you have costumes changes and props? Is your list simple: your instrument, your music, press packet and that's it? A sample audition checklist follows. Take that formula, amend it to your climate and region, and tailor it to your specific needs.

Now that we have the place to rehearse mentally and physically, how do we insure our approach is positive and constructive? When Mr. NyetGoodEnuf creeps in on little cat feet, what do you do?

Chapter 7: Summary

The definition of courage is not to be free of fear, but to walk on in spite of it.

A great deal of importance and time rests on **the physical preparation for performance. An equally important priority is your mental preparation.** Once you have the self-awareness of what works for you, you will develop a unique and very personal performance plan.

Practice visualization so it becomes natural and easy. It will make a huge difference in control and level of performance.

In your Zen studio, you will:

- Practice your plan.
- Be present to where you are right now.
- Take notes of your progress.
- Use it or lose it.
- Practice mental toughness.

More important than the length of time you have for preparation, is *how* you use your time.

Mental skills don't take the same length of practice that physical skills do, but **they are more difficult to unlearn.**

Take time off: you need refreshment.

What are you aiming for?
- You will **work toward consistency** in performance.
- You will **focus your mental and physical rehearsal**. Focus = better use of your time.
- You are aiming to attain a **degree of refinement that makes you a pro**.
- You are aiming to achieve a **level of minimum skill below** which you do not fall.

When you learn new material, **you must have a plan that utilizes the methods and skills that work best for you to make the material and the technique a part of you.**

Before the performance or audition: Go to the checklist.

Review your successful performances. What worked? What did not? Why?

Chapter 7: Exercises

Physical space preparation

As I said in the previous chapter, you need to invest yourself physically in the space in which you're going to work every day. Clarify your intention to make this a comfortable, practical and efficient workspace for you. You can transform the smallest space into a good rehearsal space You need:

- Privacy
- Comfort (seating)
- Workspace
- Storage space
- Timer or try http://www.e.ggtimer.com or www.rescuetime.com
- Video camera
- Your instrument

Paint the walls a color you like, add artwork that inspires you. Hang photos of people you love, or posters of performers you admire. A full-length mirror is a great help. Don't ever go out on stage without looking at yourself in a full-length mirror. Look at the back too. A hand mirror will do; a three-panel mirror is great. Are your shoes shined and in good shape? Is your hem hiked up in the back? Put on your honest glasses: no rose-colored ones for this exercise.

TO DO LIST	WHAT DO I NEED LIST

Mental preparation

Download the Cycle of Nine online. You can perform your own ritual for calming and stilling yourself before work. No matter what ritual you choose, make sure you do it. Make it a habit. Creating mental space for your work is vital to the quality of work you will be able to do in a shorter amount of time.

Plan time for your mental preparation. Don't fit it in haphazardly. Learn to visualize. Imagine and run through every single aspect of an audition or performance you are preparing. *Learning is a process, not an event.*

Budget your time

How long does it take you to learn a piece? Work backwards from that. Let us say you need to learn an art song and it takes you two weeks to learn it for performance. Allocate time to learn: the rhythm, the correct pronunciation of the words, expression, the translation and subtext and the melodic line. Then you have to allow time to work the song into your voice. How long does it take for you? Again, budget the time.

The benefits of working this way allow you to be calmer and more relaxed. You have broken down what you need to do into bite-size pieces and given yourself time to work on each. That relieves tension. It is no longer a huge mountain to climb. It's an incremental journey to the summit. What does your breakdown for learning look like? Sketch it out on these various timesheets. Use these and copy them for yourself or create your own. Honor your own rhythms. Do you work best in 15 min. increments, or one-hour increments? Learn that about yourself and respect it.

NOTES:

PREPARATION CHART

WHAT NEEDS TO BE LEARNED	STEPS NEEDED	TIME NEEDED

TIME USAGE CHART (example)

TIME	MON	TUES	WED	THUR	FRI	SAT	SUN
6 AM	Exercise	Sleep					
7 AM	Food						
8 AM		Practice					
9 AM	Work						
10 AM							
11 AM							
12 PM							
1 PM							
2 PM							
3 PM							
4 PM							
5 PM							
6 PM	Food						
7 PM	Play						
8 PM							
9 PM	Practice						
10 PM							
11 PM							
12 AM	Sleep						

Key Activities:

*SLEEP *REHEARSE *WORK *EAT *EXERCISE *PLAY, ETC.

TIME USAGE CHART

TIME	MON	TUES	WED	THUR	FRI	SAT	SUN
6 AM							
7 AM							
8 AM							
9 AM							
10 AM							
11 AM							
12 PM							
1 PM							
2 PM							
3 PM							
4 PM							
5 PM							
6 PM							
7 PM							
8 PM							
9 PM							
10 PM							
11 PM							
12 AM							

Key Activities:

*SLEEP *REHEARSE *WORK *EAT *EXERCISE *PLAY, ETC.

PERFORMANCE LEVEL CHART

DATE & PLACE	University Recital May 17	Charity Concert Aug 15	Carmen Performance Sept 25	Samson Performance Nov 27	Verdi Requiem NY Dec 10	New Years Eve Vienna Dec 31
PERFECT						
EXCELLENT						
VERY GOOD						
GOOD			Sick, ugh!			Champagne before I sing? Never again!
FAIR	Too nervous					
BAD						

Your goal is to be in the Good to Excellent range. It is the mark of a professional. A first ring pro is usually in the Very Good to Excellent range. Perfection happens rarely. Don't get hung up on it.

Harness Your ZEBRA

PERFORMANCE LEVEL CHART

DATE & PLACE							
PERFECT							
EXCELLENT							
VERY GOOD							
GOOD							
FAIR							
BAD							

Your goal is to be in the Good to Excellent range. It is the mark of a professional. A first ring pro is usually in the Very Good to Excellent range. Perfection happens rarely. Don't get hung up on it.

Audition Checklist

- Music/shoes/instrument/prop/sides.
- Cell phone (and iPod to close out the world).
- Address and directions of audition hall and phone contact.
- Shoes (other than the boots you're using to slosh through the snow or your flip-flops, unless you want to perform in them, it's up to you).
- Check/money for your pianist, if applicable.
- Exact bus/subway fare, if needed.
- Gas for the car.
- Check traffic on TV, your GPS or on your phone before you leave. (Allow extra time)
- Business cards.
- Press packet (head shots, resume).
- Antistatic spray in the winter (unless you're willing to take the chance of having your clothes cling tightly to your body after you remove your winter coat).
- Snacks and water.
- Hairbrush or comb.
- Makeup and mirror. Check out back and front view!
- Tissues and saline spray, or hand lotion, aromatherapy bottle, cough drops or those great Jolly Rancher candies (Marquita, how did you ever sing *Aida* with one of those lodged in your cheek?).

Design your list

AUDITION CHECKLIST	ITEM/PROCESS	DONE

Chapter 8
E is for Eliminate Your Negative Self-talk

There is no room in your mind for negative thoughts.
The busier you keep yourself with the particulars of shot assessment and execution,
the less chance your mind has to dwell on the emotional. This is sheer intensity.
- Jack Nicklaus, golf champion

Now that we have a Zen studio, we have a choice. We can fill it with negativity or positive and productive awareness. Have you noticed that about 80% of what you tell yourself is negative? Would you talk to your best friend the way you talk to yourself? Are you ready to change negative self-talk into positive affirmations? Yes? Then read on, McDuff.

Awareness is the first step
The first step in eliminating negative self-talk is awareness. You can't change something until you are aware of it.

Here's your challenge: set ten minutes on a timer and see if you can keep up with the jumble of thoughts that run through your head. Write down whatever you can or record it. Are you surprised? Do you realize what a huge percentage of your thoughts are negative?

Pick various times over the next week. Choose five minutes here, ten minutes there and pay attention to what you tell yourself. I find myself hearing old voices that sneer at me and at my abilities. I hear voices that say, "I can't." However, if the voices are telling you to go play in traffic or go kill the goldfish, see a doctor. Now.

My solution for dealing with "I can't" is to ask, "Why not?" What we are dealing with in this chapter is not just about performance or performers. Our thoughts create our lives. If we have ever had any suspicion that we are a bit of the divine, this is proof. Creativity is divine and we are all creators.

Accentuate the positive

Your thoughts and beliefs of the past have created this moment, and all the moments up to this moment. What you are now choosing to believe and think and say will create the next moment and the next day and the next month and the next year.
- Louise Hay, author of You Can Heal Your Life

For some of us, skeptical me included, merely the phrase *positive affirmation* sounds like a woo-woo invitation to your local fortuneteller. I'm here to tell you that positive affirmations work. But *they do not work unless they are accompanied by behavioral change*. In other words, you can't just sit on the edge of your bed and repeat "I am a success" 400 times and poof! You are a success. It doesn't work that way. Affirmations pave the way to action and reinforce it. It's a very symbiotic relationship. What are affirmations? They are positive statements of a desired outcome, visualization or goal. Usually they are short and very focused. By repeating or writing them many times, they replace your negative chatter. You are building new neural pathways.

I find that repeating my affirmations aloud in the morning help me to silence the negative. They give my energy and attitude a clear and positive focus. Remember this is a process and not a fast fix. Our negative thoughts are an ingrained habit. We need to unlearn the habit and replace it with the new design. It will take at least three to four weeks, perhaps more. It took a long time to ingrain the habit so be patient. Recognizing the habit is the first step.

Write a new script
Create a story that accomplishes your goals, your vision and the kind of life you want. Paint the kind of career you want and the kind of lifestyle you desire. Wrap it all into a beautiful, vivid daydream. Whenever you find your mind wandering toward "I can't," start running the tape of the script you have created.

Find pictures in magazines or online that enable you to see what your imagination has created. Create a vision board or dream board and put it in a prominent place where you can glance at it and the images become imprinted. Make your vision concrete reality. Ask yourself how you will feel when that dream becomes reality. Register, and remember, that feeling.

A client who was not happy with her career progress came to me for some fast tracking. When I asked her to write down what her perfect day would look like, she was surprised by what rose to the surface. We prepared for the exercise by doing a breath and relaxation technique so she was receptive to more than her conscious mind. (See the <u>Cycle of Nine</u>, an excellent tool for work like this.) She was sure she was on her way to footlights, world tours and standing ovations. Not so. What rose to her heart was something quite unexpected.

It's early morning and sunlight is filtering through the sheer curtains of my huge bed. My loving husband has just brought me coffee and a kiss before he goes to work. I take my coffee out to the beautiful deck and listen to the surf roll in. I bring my laptop outside and begin the third chapter of my new novel.

I'm a very popular author and the proceeds of my last three books have allowed us to purchase this gorgeous Italian villa on the shores of the Mediterranean.

I write for two hours and then go down to the beach to do my yoga. Then a shower in my gorgeous bathroom and I get ready to greet the day and the interviews. I have a Skype appointment with my director in NY for the Fresh Start Women's Centers. I have five of them now, all over the US. We continue our plans for the huge fundraiser just after Thanksgiving.

My cook has prepared a light wonderful lunch. We discuss what recipes I will create in the evening as we're having a dinner party for ten guests on our terrace.. As always, our parties ring with laughter and beauty, wonderful communication and a sense of big love. I am one happy woman, doing what I really want. I feel an enormous sense of gratitude as I close my eyes for a night of dreaming.

This is a perfect example of allowing what your heart truly wants to rise to the surface instead of doing what our parents, friends, teachers or coaches expect, or tell us we *should* want. Just because you have enormous talent for piano doesn't mean you have to be a pianist.

Write out the negative characters
Pay attention to the people around you. If your best friend has a 'poor me' attitude, keep in mind that is more infectious than a cold virus. Don't discuss your dreams, plans or affirmations with people who are unsupportive. Instead, surround yourself with people who will empower you. Get to know people who are walking toward dreams and goals: it is inspiring.

You will begin to notice we pick people who have a familiar energy dynamic as friends. Sometimes the connection isn't obvious until much later. I had a friend whom I loved dearly and couldn't figure out why she told me, fifteen years later, she had *always* been jealous of me and didn't want to be my friend anymore. I was devastated! When I looked back at the relationship, it became clear she worshipped the singer I was and was jealous of the person. My mother was exactly like that. I accepted, with open arms, a familiar energy. This can happen to any of us but learn to pay attention.

On the other side of the spectrum, people with a positive attitude affect your own attitude as well. Haven't you noticed how someone who carries a little black cloud over their heads affects the mood of an entire group? Positive people lighten the whole atmosphere.

Face your fears
Did you know most of us will stay in an uncomfortable, difficult and painful situation simply because it's familiar? We stay because we're afraid of change. We're scared of taking a chance because we might fail. Indeed, we might fail. There are no guarantees of success in any business or in any situation. Nevertheless, how do you know if it's going to be a success or failure if you don't try?

Fear of the unknown holds us back in so many instances. We are willing to lie to ourselves and try to make do or whine about what we have. We are willing to convince ourselves we're happy in our present situation. In reality, our hearts yearn for something completely different. I can't remember how many times I tell my clients: aim for what you really want, not just for what you think you can get.

Ask yourself, what is the worst that can happen? If the worst should happen, what would you do about it? Bad situations can jolt us out of our complacency. They can cause us to take risks that turn into pathways to unexpected success and fulfillment. This is one of the vital components of mental toughness – *flexibility*.

Isn't the unexpected part of the excitement and happiness of being on stage? In reality, we never know what lies around the next corner. All we can do is make a choice with our present knowledge and experience.

Stay present
You've heard the expression 'the gift of the present,' yes? You can't change the past and the present isn't here yet. All you've got is right now. The only thing you can do about the past is to change how you tell the story of your past, even to yourself.

You may need help. Get it. If your parenting was exceptionally cruel, instead of staying stuck in that pain, you can reframe the story. You can create an awareness of the challenge it was to have teachers of that magnitude beside you. You can be grateful for the strength you had to survive the abuse.

In the right now, if we practice Zen mindfulness, we can focus and transform ourselves and our work. *It does no good to obsess over what's going to happen when all we have is what is.* A great way of letting go of the future is to concentrate on the steps it takes to make our vision reality. It is far more productive to concentrate on what we need to do right now.

Common distortions
Let's look at some of the distortions in our perception that make stage fright and your dissatisfaction with yourself worse:

- You make assumptions: i.e. the person in the front row who is yawning or looking angry, absolutely hates you. It has nothing to do with you.

- If you're not perfect, you're a failure. Everything is black and white.

- You pick on one mistake and magnify that so it covers up anything positive.

- When someone tells you they enjoyed your performance, you dismiss the positive comment and think they're just being nice and lying through their teeth.

- You just know things are going to be horrible. That can be a self-fulfilling prophecy.

- You dramatize everything. That person is soooo much better than you and you are sooooo much worse. Again, there's that bugaboo of comparison.

- You "should" all over yourself. Shoulda, woulda, coulda, that leads to disaster.

The attitude of gratitude

If we could read the secret history of our enemies, we should find in each man's life sorrow and suffering enough to disarm all hostility.

-Henry Wadsworth Longfellow

Literally, take the distortions above, add your own, and put the negative things you say to yourself in one column. In another column, create an opposite statement. Voilà, that's an affirmation. You will get a chance to do just that in the exercises. Here's an example: I just know things are going to be horrible. Transform it into: I have worked very hard on this with joy and care. I'm going to have a successful performance.

John Gray wrote *How to Get What You Want and Want What You Have: A Practical and Spiritual Guide to Personal Success*. It highlights an important truth. There is not a person in the world free of difficult times. There is not a soul without any problems in their lives. It's a given. That's reality. It doesn't matter whether we like it or not. It's simply the way it is. We have a choice in how to view our reality. We can focus on the enjoyable moments or the devastating ones. A helpful community saved my friends' possessions as floodwaters rose in Australia. They could focus on the fact that the floods destroyed over 30,000 homes. Instead they are marveling at how their community has come together and each person is helping another to surmount this terrible disaster.

In any place in the world at any given time, there are natural disasters that devastate people's lives. There will always be people better off than you and people worse off. Again, that's reality. How you choose to view reality and how you choose to deal with it is what makes a difference in the quality of your life.

Your choice of how you choose to view the world is yours. Be grateful for what you have and be grateful for being part of a very privileged segment of society: a performing artist. We are remarkable, unusual beings. It takes courage to reveal the beauty, pain and dreams to which we aspire.

Take the time you need
Be aware that none of this will happen overnight. If you've been thinking negatively for most of your life, changing that pattern is going to take time, work, patience and perseverance. I have a prayer that may work for you:

Dear (Divinity-of-your-choice,) Please grant me patience and I want it right now. I don't understand why this hasn't worked for me.

All kidding aside, the suggestions above have the capability of changing your life but only if you are willing to consciously work at them. If you do, you will have greater happiness, peace and joy. You will also have a greater likelihood of fulfilling your potential, not only as a performer, but as a human.

Now you have a space to polish your potential, a place free of negative self-talk, and a place to prepare. So, what is the best way to prepare?

Chapter 8: Summary

The first step in eliminating negative self-talk is awareness.

A solution to, "I can't," is to ask, "Why not?"

Our thoughts create our lives.

Affirmation: positive statement of desired outcome, visualization or goal. Usually short and very focused.

Remember, **this is a process, not a fast fix**.

Write a new script. Create a story that accomplishes your goals and your vision. The kind of life you want. Wrap it all in a beautiful, vivid film. You can run it when fear strikes.

Create a vision board, a dream board. **Concentrate on the steps it takes to make your vision a reality**: you won't have time for anything else.

Just because you have talent for _____, doesn't mean you have to be a_____.

Don't discuss your plans or affirmations with people who are unsupportive and negative.

Most of us will stay in an uncomfortable, difficult and painful situation simply because it's familiar and we're afraid of change.

Ask for what you really want, not just for what you think you can get.

If the worst should happen, **bad situations can jolt us into taking risks that turn into new opportunities.**

Transform your common distortions. Write your negative thoughts in the left column and in the right column create your positive affirmations.

We have a choice in how to view our reality.

If you've been thinking negatively for most of your life, changing that pattern is going to take time, work, patience and perseverance.

Chapter 8: Exercises

The ZEBRA Transformation

I came up with a solution for myself that works very well to eliminate negative self-talk. Would you like to try it? Go to: www.afiartists.com and click on the link for the self-esteem bracelet. No, it's not just a cute, brightly colored bracelet: it really works when used as directed. A percentage of all proceeds from this book and products go to projects (such as Literacy Volunteers) so that every child born in the USA has an opportunity to learn how to read and write. Once that goal is achieved, we move on to the rest of the world. Would you like to be part of that?

What is keeping you off balance?

Look at the big picture first. What is bothering you? What things or situations feel like a barrier to your success? Let's make the cloudy stuff clear.

On the next page there is an example of the filled in *big picture*. Turn the page and fill in your *big picture*. Add boxes if you need to. What are your major problems? What is in your way?

Notes:

WHAT IS KEEPING YOU OFF BALANCE?
EXAMPLE

MY NEGATIVE SELF TALK

NEGATIVE SITUATIONS

- I'M AFRAID I'LL FAIL
- WHO DO YOU THINK YOU ARE?
- I DON'T KNOW HOW TO CHANGE

- FINANCES A BUMMER
- BAD ROOMAATE SITUATION
- AUDITIONS IN THE FALL, ARGG
- NOT ENOUGH REHEARSAL TIME

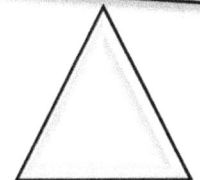

Harness Your ZEBRA

WHAT IS KEEPING YOU OFF BALANCE?
YOUR VERY OWN PITY PARTY

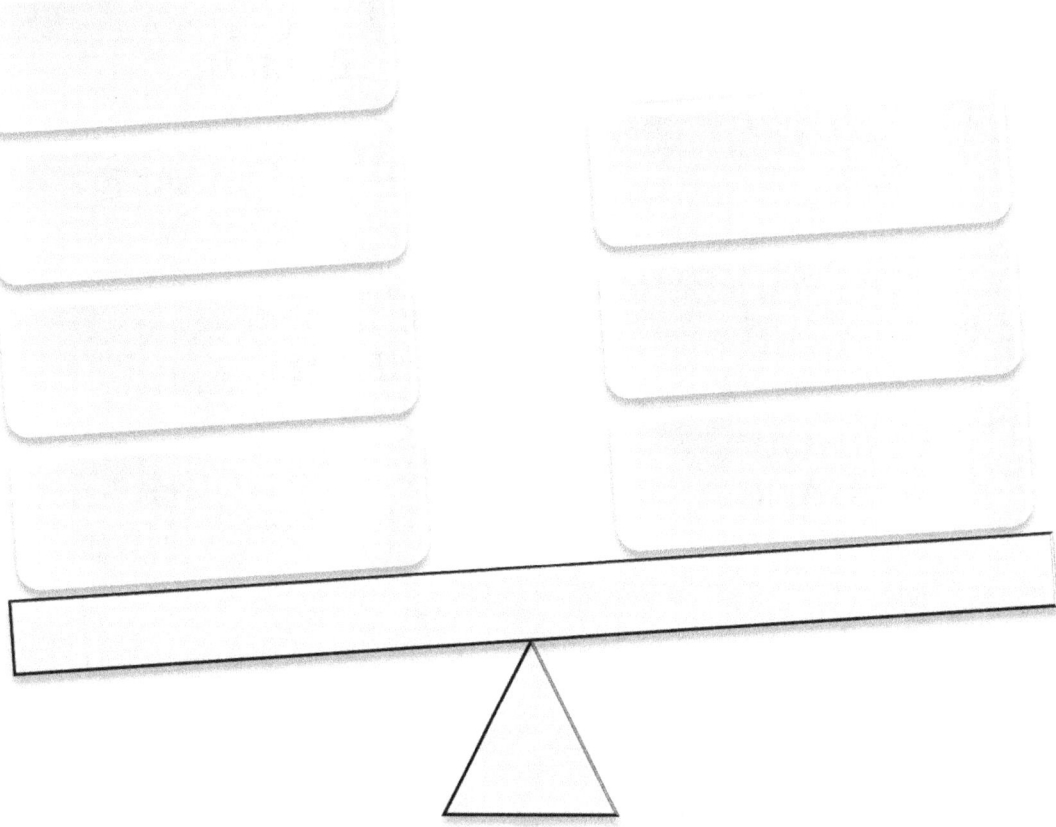

My negative dialog
Once you have filled in the unbalanced big picture, it is time for you to take out a piece of paper, tape recorder, your phone, whatever works best for you, and give yourself **five minutes of taking down the negative things you usually say to yourself.** Repeat this at least three or four times in one week. You'll be shocked at the amount of negative input we give ourselves. You have two pages of space – get going!

Notes:

My Negative Dialog → Continued

- I'm so dumb
- I can't do this!
- As always, I was bad tonight.
- Who do I think I am?
- START WRITING!

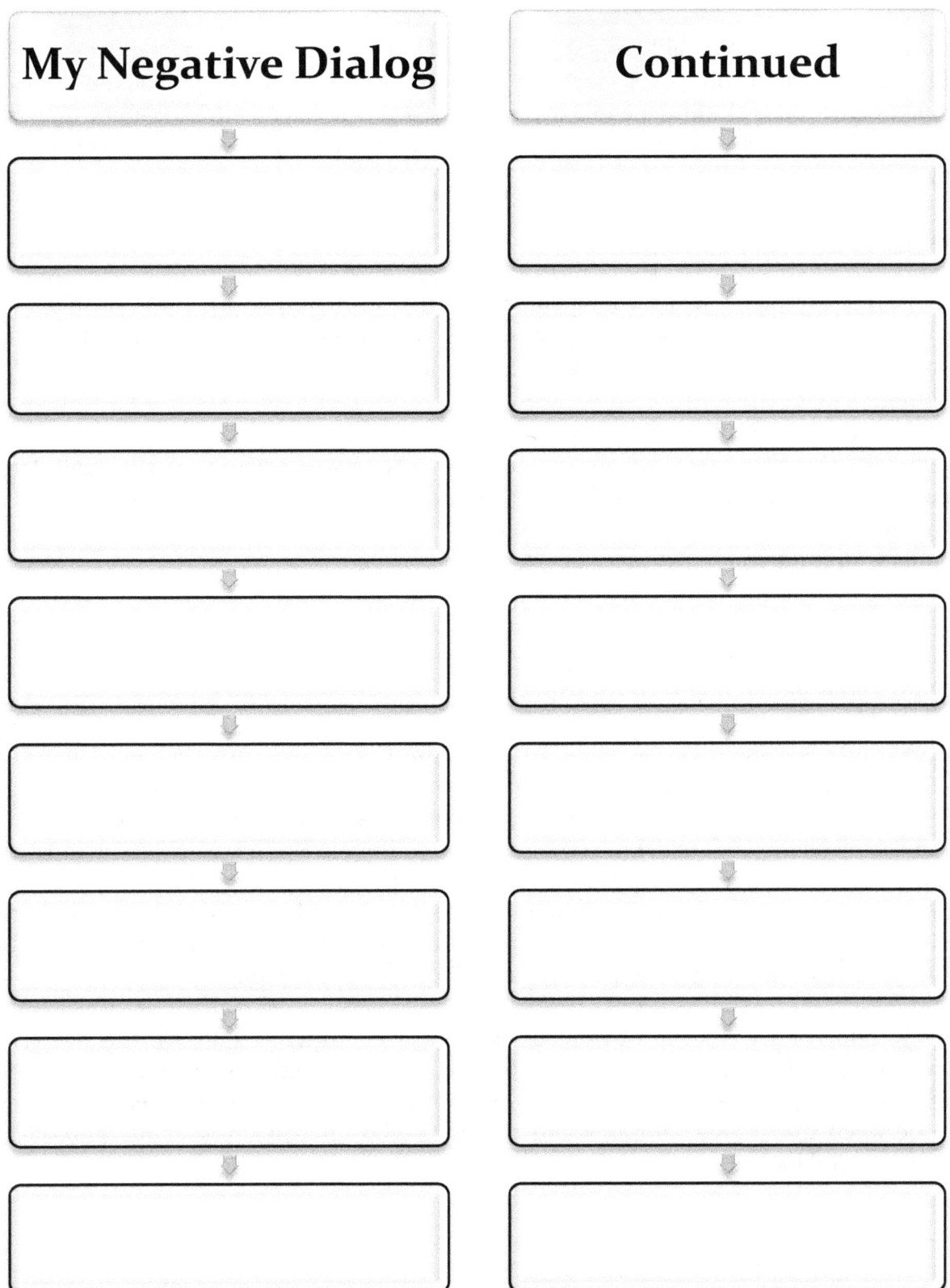

Who are the negative people in your life?

I realize you probably won't be able to get rid of all of them. You may be related to some of them. The most important thing to realize is **these people will not change**. The only way to change your interaction with these people is to change yourself. Become the change you wish to see. Make a list of these people. You can call it your S list, if you wish. You can call it anything you like – it's your list.

Likely candidates for your list:

- The energy vampires. When you spend more than 10 minutes with these people, you feel your energy has been totally sapped. You go out of your way to avoid them.
- People who are always putting you down. Most of the time they pretend they're kidding.
- People who constantly criticize you.
- Needy people who constantly make demands. They are masters of the guilt trip. You're not really doing them a favor by enabling their weakness. Think about that.
- Whiners who complain about everything.
- People who want you to fix their lives. Run!
- The list can be as long as you like. Happy list making.

Okay, so what do you do about these people? As I said, **you need to change yourself**. You need to change your interaction with these people.

For example, there is a man I know who is the Drama King of all time. When something happens to him, imagined or real, he blows it up to huge proportions. He then calls me, moans about what happened, expects me to sympathize and do something about it. He wants to enlist my energy and make me feel guilty when I don't bite his bait. That happened for about four e-mails and two telephone calls before I got the message. I nipped it in the bud. I said, I care about you a lot and I want you to be happy but I have enough drama in my life. I don't want any more. This is not my fight and this doesn't concern me. I don't want to engage with you in this way. The interaction has ended. He got the point.

Sometimes you don't have to be as obvious or as blunt, sometimes you do. Do this exercise. Think about the people who lift your spirits. Just seeing them makes your heart and mind feel better. Hearing their voice on the phone or seeing their name makes you feel good. The difference between the energy vampires and the ones who lift you up is really quite clear once you take a good look at it.

The Negative People in Your Life

THE PERSON

Example:
my friend Joe,
he's down on everything

THE SOLUTION

Minimize time together
Be honest about how I feel
Give him a chance to change

Remember Chapter 2 and the negative things you tell yourself? Make your negatives a positive using the three following diagrams. Next, take action to transform your negatives into positives. Remember, affirmations will not work unless you take action to change.

Notes:

The Effect of Negative Self-Talk on Performance

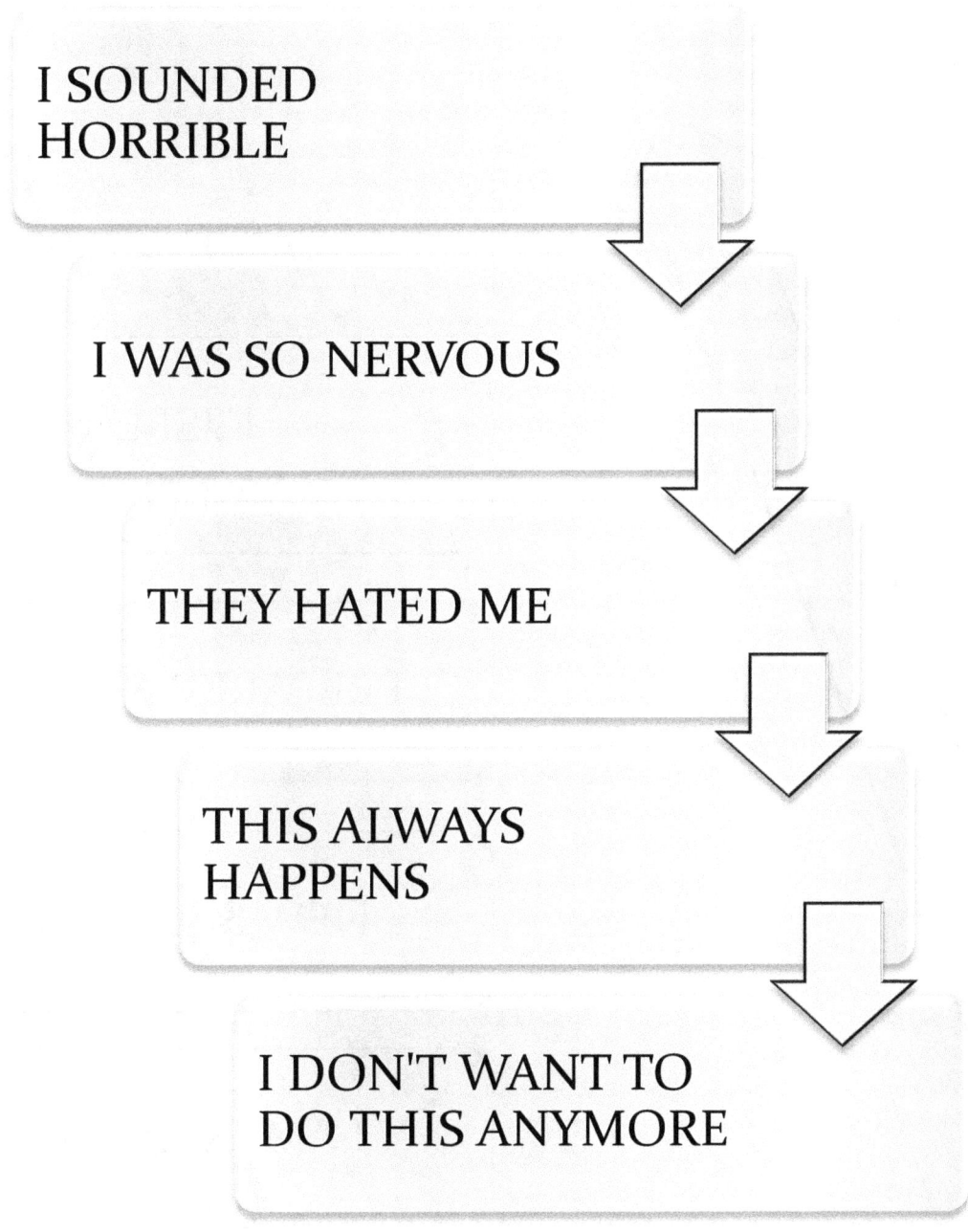

The Effects of Positive Self-Talk on Performance

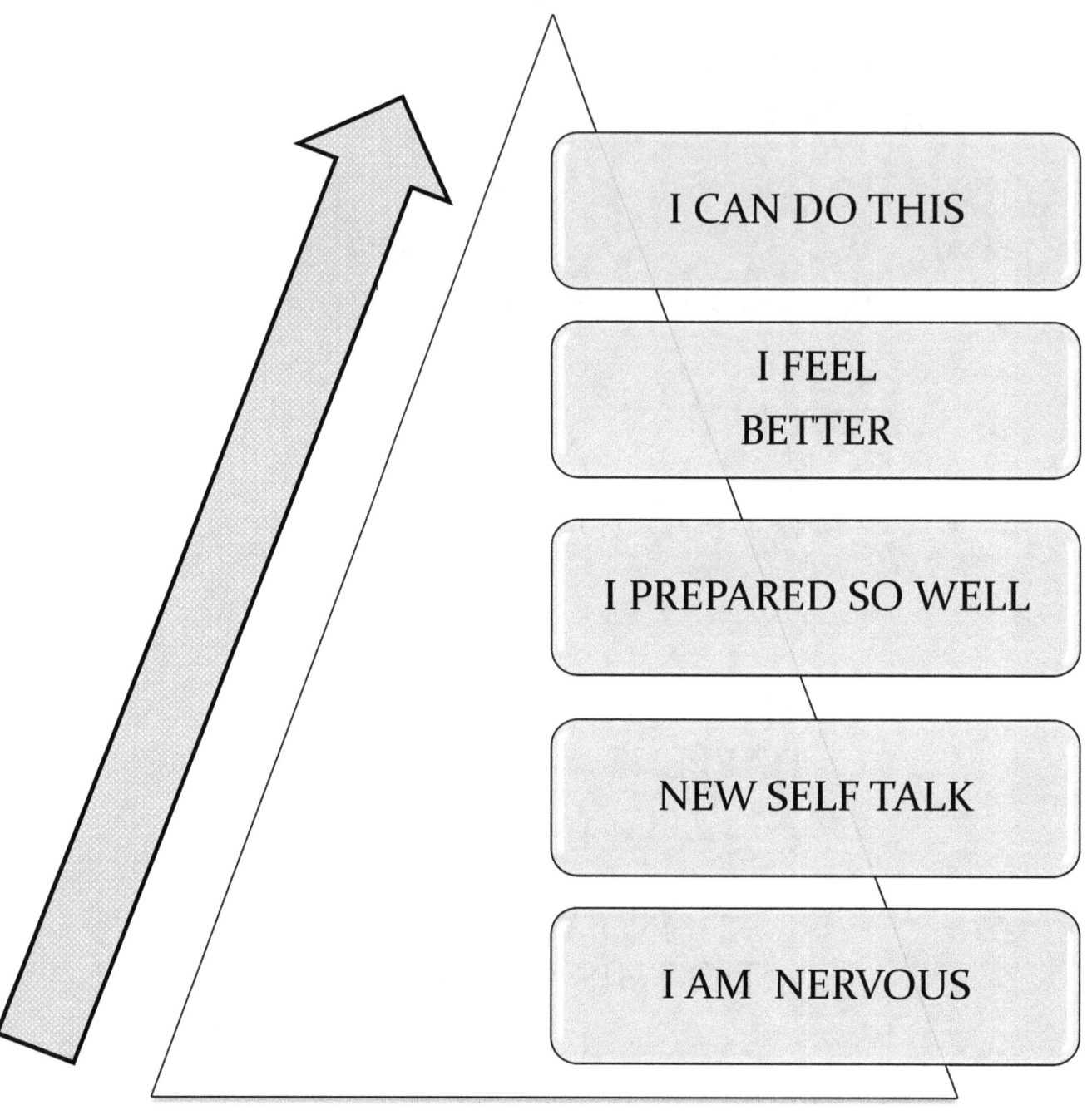

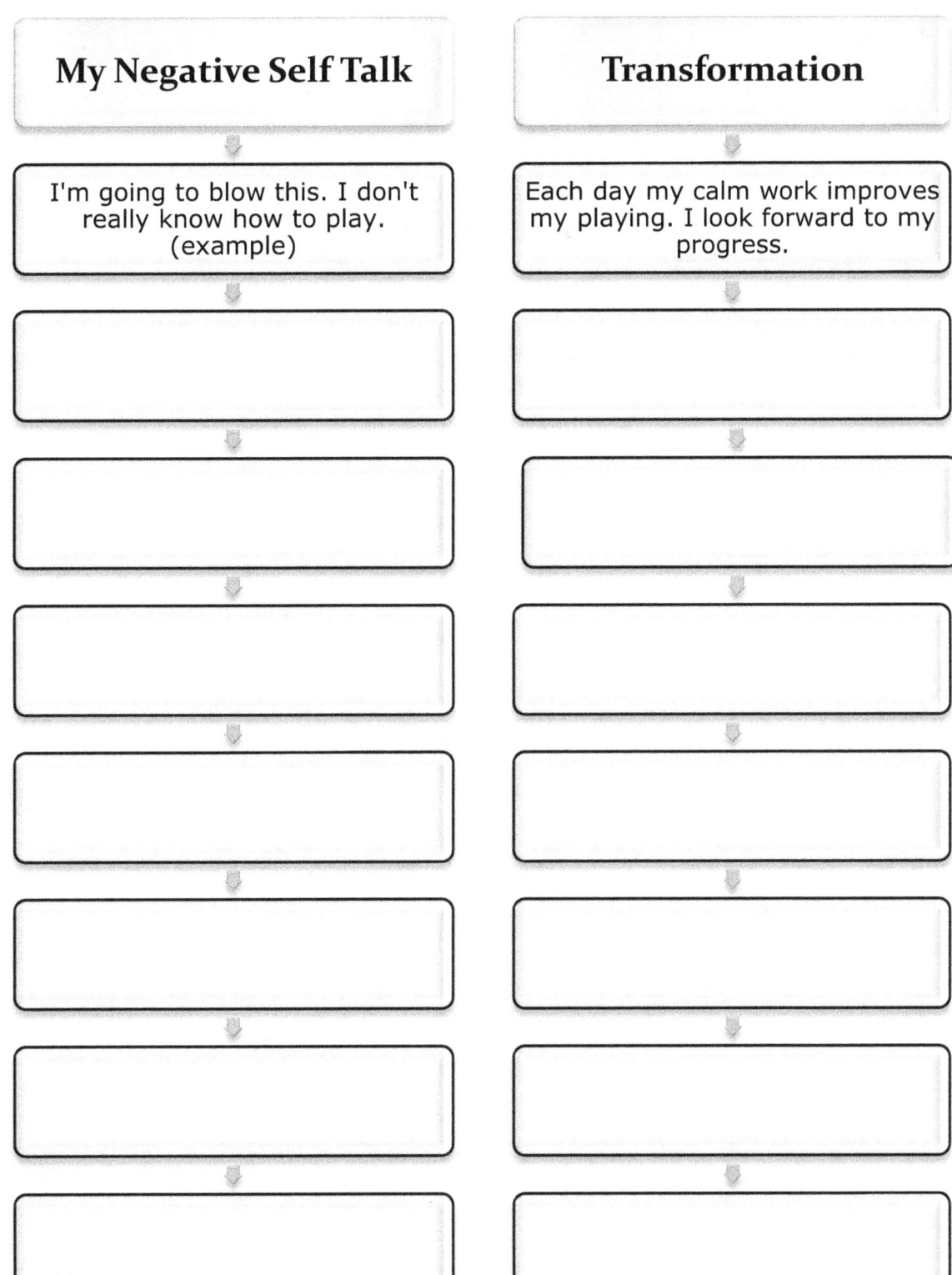

Script for burning

Now look at the off balance situations, the negative people and the negative thoughts in your life. Elaborate, exaggerate. Write yourself a dismal, dark, poor-you, pity-party version of your life.

Include the negative things you say to yourself and your horrible situation. I've given you two pages. Wallow, cry, do whatever it takes! Enjoy your misery 'cause it ain't gonna last. The only constant in the world is change.

Now for the fun part: **read it over once and burn it**! Safely. If that doesn't work for you, use it to line your parakeet's cage, or stick it under the cat litter, or tear it up into teensy-weensy pieces and flush it down the toilet. Get my drift? Lighten up. Get rid of it.

Then you will use the bracelet I mentioned to retrain your mind into following your new script.

Notes:

Negative Script For Burning
Start Writing. . .

Negative Script, Continued

For what are you grateful?
This exercise is extremely important. It affects how you view your life. Remember I said earlier, there will always be people better off than you are and people in worse condition than you. There will always be people who have more talent than you or less talent than you have. What things, situations, people, characteristics make your life worthwhile? What makes you want to get up in the morning?

Get in the habit of doing this exercise every day of your life. You can do it mentally before you pop out of bed. It will make a difference in how you view your life, your world and the situations in which you find yourself.

Instead of: nobody loves me, everybody hates me, I gotta eat a worm. How about: I feel good today. I'm healthy. I like what I have planned for my life. I have some wonderful people in my life. My job is uncomfortable right now, but it's just a means to an end. Let me read my vision once. Oh, that feels better.

Our monkey minds need a little bit of discipline to channel and utilize that fabulous energy.

Try it. You'll like it.

For What Am I Grateful? See example and keep writing. . .

My cats

- He taught me how to trust & to meow for what you want
- She taught me value of quiet dignity

Your Personal Timeline

On the next pages, there are timeline calendars to guide you to make your vision a reality. They will form the foundation for your new positive life script. Look at this as an informal business plan for your personal life. What kind of questions should you ask yourself when you fill out a ninety day, one-year or five-year plan?

- I am in this situation right now. Where do I want to be in 90 days?
- Where do I want to be 12 months from now?
- How do I see my life evolving in five years?
- What is my tolerance for my artistic career pursuit? How long will I pursue this as a career by which I make a living? What is my cutoff date?

All of these questions are merely guidelines and helpful toward analyzing a personal timeline. They are not set in stone or absolute. Ask yourself what makes sense for you.

No matter what you answer, make sure you remain flexible. Be flexible in responding to evolving and changing situations. Lighten up. New desires and aspirations may rise that weren't there thirty days ago or six months ago: pay attention to them. Think out of the box.

Take a lesson from palm trees. Although they have a very shallow root system, their flexibility makes it possible for them to survive the strongest of hurricanes.

Notes:

90 Day Planner (Example)

Dates: From _____ To _____

GET REAL

- hate where I am living

- am living above my means, change that now!

- need to get 3 experts to evaluate me within this time frame so I know how to proceed

GET CLEAR

- by end of 90 days I will be clearer on my career path

- wait to add 2nd job until I have feedback from experts

- Take online courses for virtual assistant skills – create a job with super flexibility & cash!

MONTH 1

- Give notice to landlord

- Dress rehearsal I

- contact 5 experts

MONTH 2

- Dress rehearsal II

- physical training for great appearance

- book extra coach time, confirm 3 auditions

MONTH 3

- Dress rehearsal III (with live audience)

- Take online courses

- 3 auditions for experts

GET GOING!

- increase productive practice time for auditions

- set up dress rehearsals, book space & pianist

- find another apartment, roommate?

- take or create another flexible part time job

- design one year plan with this new information

90 Day Planner

Dates: From _____ To _____

GET REAL	MONTH 1	GET GOING!
GET CLEAR	MONTH 2	
	MONTH 3	

12 Month Calendar

Dates From_____ to _____

DATE	GET REAL	GET CLEAR	GET GOING
JANUARY			
FEBRUARY			
MARCH			
APRIL			
MAY			
JUNE			
JULY			
AUGUST			
SEPTEMBER			
OCTOBER			
NOVEMBER			
DECEMBER			

5 Year Planner

Dates From _____ To _____

DATE/ TIMEFRAME	GET REAL	GET CLEAR	GET GOING
YEAR 1			
YEAR 2			
YEAR 3			
YEAR 4			
YEAR 5			

Your New Script

Go back in this chapter and read over the script that surprised my client so much. Key first step: **get yourself into a calm and centered place**. Use the *Cycle of Nine,* or whatever methods work for you. Get into a neutral and unstressed mental and physical space. From that place, allow your mind to drift into a film of your own making. You are the starring character. What is happening in your life? What are you doing? With whom are you interacting that puts a smile on your face?

Give yourself about 30 minutes. **When a new vision of your life becomes clear, take the time to write it down.** Writing it down and **reading it periodically will make your vision a reality**. It is this vision you will use to clarify the steps you need to take to get where you want to go.

Take two pages to write it out. Luxuriate, enjoy the process. *This is not an instant process, it will take time and as you learn to listen to yourself and your instincts, your script will change accordingly.* After your timeline is clear, you will write a one page summary at the end of the book.

Don't allow the "should" of your friends, family or significant others to tell you what they think you ought to do. Instead, truly get in contact with your deep instincts, your deep knowing and from that place envision what you want for your life. Not everyone dreams of his or her own yacht on the Hudson and flowing champagne. There are those who are inspired by helping others. There are those that love helping animals and the helpless creatures of this Earth.

Your **dream is the right dream for you.**

Your New Script

Your new script, continued

Chapter 9
B is for Be Prepared

*Give me six hours to chop down a tree
and I will spend the first four sharpening the axe.*
- Abraham Lincoln, American president

Is there a right way and a wrong way to prepare for performance? You bet there is. Sloppy preparation leads to sloppy performance. You need a clear method that works for you including at least two dress rehearsals. If it is good enough for Itzhak Perlman, it's good enough for you.

Work backwards
I'm serious. One of the best ways to achieve success in business, and in life for that matter, is to work backwards from the goal you envision. That's what I mean when I say: *get real, get clear, get going.*

First you need to get real. You have to be realistic about your assets and liabilities. You need to be evaluated by professionals in your business. Get real about the natural talent you have. Realistically assess the strengths and the weaknesses you possess

A friend of mine always wanted to be singer and an actor. He was tall, handsome and brilliant. No one had ever heard him sing one note and he was already 40 years old. You cannot afford to delude yourself that way. He said he was an actor but had less than a handful of professional roles and performances under his belt. He lived in self-induced poverty and spent every cent on classes and workshops. This was a brilliant man, no exaggeration here. His had a huge storehouse of theatrical knowledge. He was also a fine writer. The prison of his inertia was the dream that a spotlight would change his unhappy relationship with himself. It didn't happen.

After you get real, you have to get clear. Are you willing to harness your passion to reach your goals? You have to visualize and concretize your steps if you want to get where you want to go. Of course, that doesn't mean rigidity. It means being flexible and light and being able to dance within the constraints of very strong discipline. Once you are clear about the steps you need to take, don't think about it. Get going! Take action.

Rehearse deliberately
Most of the time, I see students rehearsing aimlessly in practice rooms. They make a mistake on a passage in the Bartok. They curse for a while and then they play it again. Instead of breaking down the mistake into elemental steps and then building it back up to speed, they simply do it all again. *Repetition without clarity about what went wrong ingrains the mistakes and anxiety too.* If you rehearse haphazardly, the linear pathways you're trying for will never become straight. Your performance will be as haphazard as your rehearsal was.

Learn it first

Dancing appears glamorous, easy, and delightful. But the path to paradise of the achievement is not easier than any other. There is fatigue so great that the body cries, even in its sleep. There are times of complete frustration, there are daily small deaths. We learn by practice. Whether it means to learn to dance by practicing dancing or to learn to live by practicing living, the principles are the same. One becomes in some area an athlete of God.

- <u>Martha Graham</u>, *dancer and choreographer*

Ironically, you can't practice the violin, until you learn how to play the violin. You can't practice singing until you learn how to sing. I wondered when I first went to Italy to work with Sara Sforni-Corti, a magnificent vocal technician and musician, why she didn't want me to go back to my rooms and practice. She said I wasn't ready until I knew what I was doing, and could understand and correct it when I did something wrong.

This may sound simple, but I assure you it's absolutely true. Unless you know how to implement the new technique you're learning, you're going to waste a lot of time. You also need to know how to warm up or practice the phrase properly or you can hurt muscles – just like an athlete.

Learn from the best

When I was growing up and studying music, I didn't have *YouTube* to reference. But for heaven sakes, if you're going to listen to *YouTube*, listen to the experts of the past. Not to imitate, but to learn. If you're going to listen to a fledgling student, who has put up her video of *Glitter and Be Gay* - mistakes and all for the world to hear, you'll only be learning bad habits. Don't do it.

Don't listen to recordings until you have learned a piece and you're beginning to master it. Then you can listen to several different interpretations and allow them to influence you. But if you copy Horowitz, you will only be a poor imitation of Horowitz, not the unique, individual you.

Learn it by heart

This is one of the basic elements of pre-performance preparation. You need to know your routine, your song, your piece cold. If the conductor says "Take it from orchestra 43," you need to know exactly where that is.

It makes no sense to bother with other preparation until you know your performance pieces with absolute certainty. Suppose you're working on dialogue that is particularly tricky or difficult to say. Work backwards. Start with the last line and keep adding to the sentence until you've memorized that, and so on and so forth. Learn it paragraph by paragraph, musical line by musical line.

Find methods to help your rote memorization. *Learn the part do not memorize it.* I deliberately picked the word rote because as an actor and as a singer, if you give preset line readings, or preset musical readings, your performance ceases to be a living thing. There is the danger of cookie-cutter performances, i.e., "I always do it this way." No matter how well you memorize something, you can never recreate the emotion of a previous moment. You can never recreate an exact performance. It needs to be a living thing.

Ideally, your interpretation is *acting truthfully in the moment within a make-believe situation* (the definition of acting). Don't memorize your readings and your interpretation. Instead, learn the beats, the silences, the words, the tonality, the key changes, or the physical sensation of a *plié* that leads into a pirouette.

Knowing what it is you need to do and then infusing it with spontaneous life is what brings a performance to inspiring heights. After removing the scaffolding of technique used in preparation, we can reveal the beauty of the creation.

Normal preparation
With experience and experimentation, you will discover what you need to prepare for any performance. You will learn the rituals you need for your day of performance. You will learn if you have food allergies, which foods to avoid for as long as a week before performance. They will slow down your reflexes or muddy your inspiration.

You need to know how you're going to get to the performance site. You need to know exactly how long that takes, with or without, traffic. You need to be sure what you're going to wear is *absolutely comfortable,* and you will look your best. The only way to do that is dress rehearsals.

This is a plan you'll use most of the time because things go wrong. That is normal. Most of the time as a professional performer, you will be performing at less than your optimum. This is due to jet lag, strange foods, allergies, low energy, breaking up with your mate and a thousand other situations that life throws our way.

On top of personal problems, you could get off at the wrong stop or miss a train. Or all of a sudden the pianist you have worked with is ill and you end up with a pianist you've never met who can't play your music. Once at an Opera North audition, I had a pianist who couldn't play Act IV of *Aida*, or an aria from *Werther* (standard opera repertoire for a mezzo). Even the *Habanera* was a stretch for him. No, I did not give a good audition. The auditioners didn't care. *Merde* happens!

Emergency preparation
You need to have a backup plan for when everything goes wrong. You may have to warm up on the subway, or on the street. You might forget your shoes and have to sing in your snow boots or your flip-flops. You need to know what your absolute minimum of preparation is. You need to know if you need a whole day, a half a day or just an hour to prepare and plan accordingly.

Personal experience
A prepared artist has everything they need with them and stays flexible. I proved that point to myself when I was on the way to Florida Grand Opera's school performance of Menotti's, *The Medium*. Baba had become one of my favorite roles, although she scared the wits out of me in the beginning. On the Palmetto Expressway heading south, traffic screeched to a standstill. We started inching forward, bit by bit, but there was no way off the Expressway where I was located. I knew I would never have time to warm up, put on my makeup and walk on stage in time for curtain.

To make matters worse, I was driving a stick shift. In the idle time, I laid out my makeup on the seat and began Mme. Flora's face. I am quite positive, judging by the expressions in his rearview mirror, that the man in front of me had never seen a woman put on so much makeup and become so increasingly ugly. Long story short, I got Baba together and arrived literally, three minutes before curtain.

How the pros do it
Contemporary composer, Michael Colgrass recounts in an article in *Music Magazine* from the early 1980s a story of famed violinist Itzhak Perlman:

Mr. Perlman role-played his Carnegie debut in his own living room. First, he set a date for the mock concert debut, and then started working toward this date with all the daily practice and general preparation he would put in for the real event. When the given day arrived, he practiced lightly, took a rest, then put on his tux and watched the clock for his eight o'clock appearance.

He warmed up in his kitchen, which he had designated as the artist's dressing room, and a few minutes before eight, waited in the wings between his kitchen and living room. Then he imagined someone saying to him, "Okay. Mr. Perlman, you're on," and he walked on stage, acknowledged the imaginary audience and played his recital, just the way he would do it in the real debut. He said he was very nervous for this mock concert and that there was no difference to him between this imaginary setting and Carnegie Hall. When the actual debut took place, he knew what stresses to expect because he had ferreted out the unknowns.[1]

This is exactly what I mean by a dress rehearsal. Ideally, you can have several dress rehearsals. It is imperative you have at least one. You must wear what you're going to wear, sleep how you need to sleep and eat what you need to eat. Then you must perform without stopping, as if you were on stage with a very real audience.

This is why the refuge of your Zen studio is so effective. Our bodies do not know the difference if we are merely visualizing, or actually doing, something. That is how vivid our creative mind is. That is why elite athletes use visualization so extensively. We need to take a page from that book.

Mr. Perlman's willingness to go through the entire process is the very least we can ask of ourselves. If it's good enough for a professional of that magnitude . . . need I say more?

Can you be too prepared?
Beware of becoming so relaxed or so on automatic that you cease to be alive in the moment. If you have no nerves, no fluttering, no excitement at all, you could have a bland, uninspired performance. The first person who has to be inspired is you.

This same composer, Michael Colgrass, had to deliver a talk before one of his orchestral pieces premiered at Carnegie Hall. The importance of the theater made him nervous.

The day of the concert was a madhouse and I got little rest or proper food (typical of the performers life on the road), so when concert time came I was edgy and tired. My piece was last on the program. At intermission I went back to the green room . . . stood on my head and wiggled my toes, which made me giggle. Then I did some mime exercises. By now the second half of the concert had started, and the orchestra was playing a Haydn symphony, so I danced to the minuet and thought to myself, "I wonder what the audience would think if they could see me now." Then I washed my face, went downstairs and stood in the wings. I felt energetic and ready, but not nervous, and the talk went well.

This exercise had circulated my blood and awakened me, but, more importantly, I had changed my image of Carnegie Hall. In this most venerable of concert halls you are supposed to be dignified, sophisticated – and scared. You don't frolic around giggling like a kid. Almost without knowing it, I had broken old associations with that hall and made new ones.[2]

Find your traditions. Find the preparation routines that work best for you. *Find the routines that allow you to thrive as an artist, and which respect your needs and your timelines.*

Through all of this preparation to truly do your best, you need to be relaxed. I don't mean sleepy and lolling on the couch. I mean not tense, pliable, alert and flexible. Come; explore how to do that with me.

Chapter 9: Summary

Sloppy preparation leads to sloppy performance.

To achieve success in business and in life, **work backwards from the goal you envision.**

Be realistic about your assets and liabilities. Get real about the natural talent you have.

Take action. Get real, get clear and get going.

Repetition without clarity about what went wrong **imprints both mistakes and anxiety.**

If you practice without knowing how to implement the new technique you're learning, **you're going to waste a lot of time and get discouraged.**

Practicing new techniques without guidance can hurt muscles.

Don't listen to a recording or watch a video until you have learned a piece. If you do, you'll be a poor imitation, not your unique self.

Know your routine, your piece, absolutely cold. **Don't bother with other preparation until you know your performance pieces.**

No matter how well you memorize something **you can never re-create the emotion of a previous moment. That is why live theater is so exciting. That moment in time never returns.**

Normal preparation: What do you need to prepare well for any performance?

Emergency preparation: What is the absolute minimum you need? Backup plan?

Have at least two dress rehearsals. Wear what you're going to wear and get the sleep you need. Eat what nourishes *you*, and then perform without stopping, as if you are on stage with a real audience.

Find your traditions. Find the preparation that work best for you. **Find the routines that allow you to thrive as an artist, and which respect your needs and your timelines.**

Our bodies do not know the difference if we are visualizing or actually doing something. Elite artists and athletes use visualization all the time.

Beware of becoming so relaxed that you cease to be alive in the moment. **You need to be inspired to inspire an audience.**

Exercises: Chapter 9

How do you prepare?
Use the following schedules to design your personal, customized schedule for one week prior to a performance or audition and two weeks prior.

Remember to work backwards from your goal. For example, if I need to be at my coach's studio in Manhattan on West 72nd St & West End at 11AM, I arrange my schedule this way:

- Arrive at destination 20 min early, time for a coffee (and a mint for coffee breath?)
- Subway #2 express from 42nd St by 10:15AM
- 99S Bus from Jersey City at 9AM
- Bus stop by 8:45AM
- Leave for bus stop 8:30AM
- Breakfast & get ready 7:30AM
- Get up at 7AM, journal

Your one-hour coaching session has taken *six hours* of your time! Adjust the above plan to your city and your travel mode. Yes, there is a lot of time "wasted" to get to an appointment at 11AM. Our logical minds can't quite accept that so we are often late. Don't be – work backwards and use that time to practice visualization.

Use your travel time
In the paragraph above, I talked about public transportation but it's the same if you are driving. Listen to the pros play or sing your pieces in the car. Get to know the entire work you are practicing, not just your excerpt. Listen to an audio book, perhaps a biography of the composer or lyricist.

Take every opportunity to deepen and broaden your knowledge. The ten thousand hours it takes to make you an expert can be absorbed in many ways. Don't neglect transportation time.

Keep a recording device or your phone to "jot down" your thoughts, ideas and reminders. Keep your files in one place, so you can find them when you need them.

No, you can't do this while you're driving. Use the travel time to visualize each step, each sound and each moment of your coming performance. If you do so intensely enough, your actual performance will feel like déjà vu.

Week II Prior to <u>CHARITY PERFORMANCE</u> *(example)*

DATES <u>_SEPT 12 – SEPT 18_</u>

DAY 1
- Go to Secaucus & check out gown sale (be there by 10AM)
- Work on program 2 hrs

DAY 2
- Rehearsal with coach in city
- Finish program notes

DAY 3
- Change encore
- Clean up memorization, 3 hrs

DAY 4
- Increase yoga to 1 hour
- Work with pianist & confirm 2 run throughs

DAY 5
- Exercise, vocalize
- Run program without stopping, video

DAY 6
- Pick up dress from dressmaker (got perfect shoes, yay!)
- Dress rehearsal 1 for my cat, video. Queenie gave me a gold star, :-)

DAY 7 - REST

Week II Prior to _____

DATES _____

DAY 1

DAY 2

DAY 3

DAY 4

DAY 5

DAY 6

DAY 7 - REST

Week I Prior to *CHARITY PERFORMANCE* (example)

DATES *Sept. 19 - 25*

DAY 1
- Polish program, words, tricky spot in Colgrass' *New People*
- Dentist for pearly smile
- Confirm video & audio people

DAY 2
- Watch previous videos, take notes
- Dress II with David M.

DAY 3
- Facial & massage
- Mental run through
- Many short warm-ups

DAY 4
- Final dress with David M.

DAY 5
- OFF!

DAY 6
- Performance

DAY 7 – ~~REST~~ **Party!!**

Week 1 Prior to _____

DATES _____

DAY 1

DAY 2

DAY 3

DAY 4

DAY 5

DAY 6

DAY 7

Performance Day Schedule

As a leading lady, I had a lot of responsibility resting on my shoulders and I needed a whole day to get ready for an opera.

- I awoke early, drank warm water with ½ lemon squeezed into it.
- Did yoga and meditation (60-90 min).
- Had a great breakfast; heavy on protein and light on carbohydrates.
- I went over my score, silently, note by note, word by word (no matter how many times I had performed the role).
- If the role was new, I walked through the staging.
- I did something mindless: watched TV, read a magazine.
- Had a very light lunch: salad with protein.
- Began warming up vocally, in 10-15 min increments.
- Packed my theater bag, water, snacks, score, and accessories.
- Visualized my performance from beginning to end, correcting the mistakes.
- Had a steak and salad around 4PM.
- Rested, showered.
- Theater by 5PM for 8PM curtain.
- By 5:30PM, my charts were on the wall for each act (costumes, accessories, props), my foundation was on and the character was coming to life.

Design your list

PERFORMANCE CHECK LIST: TIME	ITEM/PROCESS	DONE

Chapter 10
R is for Relaxation & Ritual

The autonomic nervous system is divided into the sympathetic system, which is often identified with the fight-or-flight response, and the parasympathetic, which is identified with what's been called the relaxation response. When you do yoga - the deep breathing, the stretching, the movements that release muscle tension, the relaxed focus on being present in your body - you initiate a process that turns the fight-or-flight system off and the relaxation response on. That has a dramatic effect on the body. The heartbeat slows, respiration decreases, blood pressure decreases. The body seizes this chance to turn on the healing mechanisms.

- Richard Faulds, English sport shooter

Relaxation and ritual prepare you for excellent work. In this brief clip of Faulds you will be amazed to see such exquisite relaxation in the way he holds the rifle. Look at the way he aims and shoots. It's astounding! Have you seen the effortless leaps of ballet legend Jacques D'Amboise? What relaxes you? Do you meditate? Do yoga? T'ai Chi, exercise? Do you listen to music that you love, dance, run and stretch?

What is relaxation?
Let us define what relaxation is in relation to a performer. Webster's describes *relax* as: 1) make less compact to make less tense or rigid, 2) to make less severe or stringent, 3) to make soft or enervated, 4) to relieve from nervous tension.

Three of these qualities are essential to performers. Number three of the definition, "to make soft or enervated," is the last thing we want. The first definition, "to make less tense or rigid" is both valid and essential. As performers, we need a certain amount of muscular tension and contraction to execute our craft. If we were completely free of tension and contraction, we would probably be limp and asleep. What we want instead is relaxation that allows fluid contraction and release. This will help us to better our performances as singers, dancers, actors and musicians. Nervous tension is death to good performance. So how do we find this balance?

Anyone can learn conscious relaxation if they view it as an essential part of their performance toolbox. Optimum conditions allow for relaxation, which cannot exist at the same time as worry and anxiety. Yet there must be enough arousal and focused tension for high-level performance.

Medically, relaxation in the form of biofeedback training, behavioral therapy, and meditation can physically lower blood pressure, decrease insomnia and lower blood cortisol levels. It can, increase serotonin in the brain, ease migraines, help digestion and even PMS. There are measurable changes in our brain waves when we are relaxed. So, does relaxation help performance? You bet.

Our body and mind work in a naturally cyclical way. Unless we take a break from extreme concentration and work, we lose our point. We become irritated and lose our perspective. We become stressed and even lower our resistance to disease.

Physical relaxation

There are so many ways to relax physically, enough to choose what delights you. Make up your own list.

- Dance.
- Walk.
- Garden.
- Play with pets.
- Play sports or games.
- Make love.

Make sure you choose a physical exercise that strengthens your core. Core strength is vital for all performers. Try out <u>Callenetics,</u> a great way to re-shape and strengthen your body. Your core muscles are the ones around your trunk and pelvis. With core strength you will have better breath support, balance, stability and nicer looking abs. Dancers get it. Wise up: it's invaluable.

Mental relaxation

- Listen to music.
- Switch off technology.
- Watch TV.
- Meditate.
- Spend time with friends.
- Listen to nature.
- Do nothing.
- Read.
- Laugh.

The best form of relaxation is one that involves both physical and mental aspects. Yoga is an extraordinary tool for a performer. It requires a full range of movement and depth of attention. Depending on the kind of yoga you choose, the focus is on breath and the stretching and lengthening of muscles.

Personal experience

My introduction to yoga was through a dear friend and colleague: Kate handed me Richard Hittleman's, *Yoga: 28 Day Exercise Plan*. This small paperback turned out to be a lifesaver and traveled all over the world with me. Because of my travel and performance schedule, I was unable to work with a teacher. Sometimes I was on the road for six to ten months in a year. I needed something that worked for me without equipment. By simply placing a towel on the floor - poof! Instant gym.

The rewards of my daily yoga practice were so extraordinary that I cannot stress enough how important exercise is to your level of performance. Yehudi Menuhin, famed violinist and conductor, stated that his yoga teacher, BKS Iyengar, taught him how to play the violin because of the relaxation he discovered when he practiced yoga.[1]

Part of the reason I was so in demand as a performer was that my body was flexible, strong and able to meet the rigors of the characters I portrayed. I could slide down the length of Samson's body and up again and my sound never wavered. I clambered down scaffolding from 30 feet in the air during a controversial Australian production. I was singing the Habanera at the time. That kind of core strength is valuable for any performer.

Out of our headspace

The performing violinist continually reviews the hours, days and weeks preceding a performance, charting the many elements that will release his potential ... he knows that when his body is exercised, his blood circulating, his stomach light, his mind clear, the music ringing in his heart, his violin clean and polished, its strings in good order, the bow hair full and evenly spread, then - but only then - he is in command...
— Yehudi Menuhin, violinist and conductor

Exercise can take us out of our heads and into a greater awareness of our physicality. It distracts us from worry and gives us a sense of contentment with our accomplishment. Then, our natural drugs, like serotonin, and endorphins kick in – no prescription needed.

We are ahead of the game if we realize that relaxation is every bit as important as effort. Happy, healthy, balanced people take the time to learn what relaxes them and make it a priority. Our work as performers is very demanding. So I stress the importance of putting relaxation at the top of our list, right up there along with practice and learning.

It's wonderful that we have 24/7 availability of cell phones, internet, e-mails and texts, but the chronic stress of constant communication can lead to serious problems. Give yourself a break.

What is best for you?
I have not gone into the particulars of any specific exercise or activity, because all of these solutions are valid. What matters is how much you love the activity you choose. *If you don't love it and the rewards are not tangible, you will not have the discipline to keep it up.*

Find what works for your body and mind. Try a free dance class. Take up fencing or start running. Rescue a dog and take it for walks three times a day. Check out local resources like your Chamber of Commerce, grocery bulletin boards, and university Continuing Education classes. Google "Free classes." If you are able, get a private yoga instructor. Take flamenco classes and drive your apartment neighbors mad!

If you are traveling, remember your relaxation ritual or exercise must be portable. Your rewards are waiting – move!

The Cycle of Nine
How about a mini vacation to ease your stress? You do not have to go anywhere or use any equipment. All you need is yourself, your breath, and less than four minutes total for a wonderful exercise called the <u>Cycle of Nine</u>. Try a downloadable MP3 *Cycle of Nine* for your phone or computer.

I have had many interesting experiences in my life as I traveled the globe. One of them was meeting a Thai monk who had lived in a monastery for thirty years and left to join the secular world. He was a fascinating man and was a specialist in Thai massage.

I wish I could say I took the essence of this wonderful healer and put it in a capsule. You would be able to take it this evening and by morning, be totally stress-free. Unfortunately, that is not the case. Most worthwhile things happen in increments.

Benefits
I promise you that the refreshment of these few minutes will surprise you on many levels. You will notice increased mental clarity. You will notice your neck feels longer and the muscles in your shoulders have relaxed enormously. You will be amazed at how much we hold our breath and how much we tense muscles when working, especially at a desk.

One of the reasons why orchestral conductors have such tremendous stamina and usually live until a ripe old age is because of their constant upper body workout. Their breath use and the use of their arms is similar to what a baby does when it cries. A baby uses its diaphragm and is breathing perfectly. It's also usually flailing its little arms around.

When you learn to breathe more fully, you will notice even your speaking voice will feel and sound different. You are utilizing your core and belly breathing, not merely the shallow breathing that most of us do day in and day out.

So how is the _Cycle of Nine_ done properly? There are three steps for preparation:

1. Stand up and get into a nice neutral position. Neutral position is: feet facing straight ahead shoulder width apart,. Your knees are slightly bent and relaxed. Your ankles and your hipbones are aligned. You've corrected your sway back by tilting the pelvis up just a bit.

2. Lift your shoulders to your ears. Roll them back and drop them down. That opens your chest around the sternum. Feel the expansion in your rib cage? If seated, make sure your feet are flat on the floor and your hands are relaxed on your thighs. Do the same thing as when you're standing up. Lift your shoulders to your ears without using your arms, roll them back and drop them down. Do you feel the opening in your chest?

3. Standing or seated, place your thumb on your navel and your hand softly on the space between your navel and the top of your pubic bone. As you breathe, let your hand move softly in and out. As you breathe in your abdominal muscles will expand (your belly button will move out). As you release the breath or exhale, the abdominal muscles will contract (your belly button will move in) and come in back toward the spine.

With this simple prep above, you are ready to perform the _Cycle of Nine_.

I. Stand, or seat yourself comfortably in a chair. Open your eyes and gaze at the midpoint of a wall or at the horizon.

Breathe in through your nose and exhale with an audible sigh through your mouth.

Again, breathe in through your nose and exhale with an audible sigh through your mouth.

Again, breathe in through your nose and exhale with an audible sigh through your mouth.

II. Close your eyes.

Breathe in through your nose and exhale with an audible sigh through your mouth.

Again, breathe in through your nose and exhale with an audible sigh through your mouth.

Again, breathe in through your nose and exhale with an audible sigh through your mouth.

III. Open your eyes again and gaze at the midpoint of a wall or the horizon.

Breathe in through your nose and exhale with an audible sigh through your mouth.

Again, breathe in through your nose and exhale with an audible sigh through your mouth.

Again, breathe in through your nose and exhale with an audible sigh through your mouth.

Doesn't that feel wonderful? It's simple, immediate, and you can do it anywhere. Make it a habit. You be surprised at all the benefits you'll experience. If you are ready for sleep, begin and end with eyes closed. Now, let's get into ritual.

What is ritual?
When I talk about ritual, I don't have midnight, witches, or crossroads in mind. I'm talking about habits. Habits that you have tried and tested and are quite sure work for you. For example, if you are one of the fortunate ones (remember, you are an athlete) who is able to eat three pounds of pasta before the big event, sleep for four hours and be in tip top shape for performance, then that is exactly what you need to do. If you find that eating four green apples in a row works for you, then that is what you do.

Get the idea? A ritual or a habit is not what works for anyone else. You can get your basic framework from what works for the experts and build your own ritual from that. It doesn't matter whether someone else understands it, whether they approve of it, or even like it. It's yours!

Plan ahead but be flexible
A word of warning: your ritual must be flexible. Life happens. If we become obsessed and completely dependent on our routines we will be unable to act if a single item goes wrong. The purpose of ritual is to create a comfortable framework, a controllable support method that allows us to relax and be focused.

Here's a perfect example. Let's say you always have two bananas and some walnuts before performance because it's light and nourishing. You have some carbohydrates and you have some protein. However, this afternoon there are no bananas to be found and your roommate ate the walnuts.

Okay, you set out to look for - and I don't mean five minutes before you need them – some carbohydrates and some protein. You'll have to make do this evening with some apples and some almonds. Or grab a slice of whole wheat bread with some peanut butter You could have some cashews, or some pasta with some diced chicken. Get my drift?

Okay, you have comfortable habits. You've rehearsed in your Zen studio. You have performed your relaxation exercises, and you're prepared. Last, but certainly not least, "act as if." What do I mean by that? Go to the next chapter.

Chapter 10: Summary

Relaxation and ritual prepare you for excellent work.

Nervous tension is death to good performance. **Anyone can learn conscious relaxation** if they care enough to view it as an essential part of their performance toolbox.

Physical relaxation: choose what works for you.

Make sure you choose a physical exercise that strengthens your core.

Mental relaxation: The best form of relaxation is one that **involves both physical and mental aspects.**

Relaxation is every bit as important as effort.

Happy, healthy, balanced people take the time to learn what relaxes them and make it a priority.

Whatever you choose, make sure you love the activity. **If you don't love it, and the rewards are not tangible, you will not have the discipline to keep it up.**

If you are traveling, remember, **your relaxation and exercise rituals must be portable.**

For a downloadable *Cycle of Nine* for your phone or iPod: go to www.afiartists.com

A ritual or habit is not what works for anyone else. You can get your basic framework for what works from the experts - build your own from that.

Exercises: Chapter 10

Warm ups

The stretches that follow are perfect for releasing tension and performance preparation. No matter if you are a singer, actor, dancer or instrumentalist, you get tense. Do these exercises and the tightness will roll away.

Body shaping

My favorite series of exercises are *Callenetics*. They look like they are easy. Not so, they are killers and they work. They will literally transform your body – visibly - in 10 hours. That's no idle claim. A word of warning: do not do these exercises just before you sing. I did them to show colleague how they worked just before a concert in Dubai. I had to sing *Dunque io son* the duet with all the runs from *Barber of Seville* and I had no trills or flexibility! My abdominals were so tired I was mush.

Richard Hittleman's book, *Yoga: 28 Day Exercise Plan*

Take fencing, dance or tai chi but s-t-r-e-t-c-h those muscles. The more supple you are, the more beautifully you will perform.

Mental relaxation

Meditation
Prayer
Breathing exercises

Physical alignment

Massage
Yoga
Exercise
Chiropractic
Alexander Technique
Feldenkrais

Stretches for Performance Health

1. **HEADS UP:** Stretch chin to the ceiling -- pull to the count of 5, relax, repeat 3 times

2. **HEADS DOWN:** Clasp your hands on the back of head -- pull head toward chest -- count to 5, repeat 3 times.

3. **PROFILE:** Correct body alignment, turn head toward shoulder, lift chin straight up and stretch neck -- count to 5. Repeat on other side. Do 3 times on each side.

4. **HEAD N' SHOULDERS:** Head to side -- pull head toward shoulder and count to 5 -- relax, repeat on other side. Do twice on both sides. Note: for added stretch, place opposite arm close to body and extend hand parallel to the floor.

5. **HEAD ROLLS:** Drop head toward chest -- rotate head to a count of 16 and stretch neck as you go. Reverse it.

6. **LEAKY TIRES:** Elevate shoulders to ears, don't use your arms to help, roll them back. Tense for 10 counts and then release gradually with audible breath (sssssssssss) -- relax. Repeat 3 times.

7. **PENCIL SHOULDERS:** Roll shoulders both ways, perfect circles. Do not let the arms get involved.

8. **TURTLE TUCKS:** Chin tucks -- push neck against stiff high collar, hold for count of 5 and release <u>up</u>, not out. Repeat 3 times.

9. **GO FORTH & BE!** Shoulder placement -- up, back down -- leave 'em there.

NOTE: Breathe though each exercise. Don't hold your breath and relax those knees. Do not ever yank, push or be rough with your muscles, *release each move and each muscle with your breath*. LET your body stretch, do not force it! These exercises should make you feel refreshed and ready to work.

Chapter 11
A is for 'Act as if'

It's all make believe, isn't it?
- Marilyn Monroe, actress

When you were a child, did you ever play make-believe? Isn't that part of the fun of being on stage? Let's learn a few techniques that lead you back to the joy of performance. How about a clear method to kick stage fright out the door once and for all? Are you ready to unfold your own myth? Are you ready to "act as if?" Can you visualize yourself enjoying a detailed, excellent performance? "Act as if" with true commitment and your performance will almost feel like déjà vu.

Can you whistle?

Rodgers and Hammerstein in *The King and I* wrote one of the greatest recommendations for conquering stage fright and for facing uncomfortable situations in our lives. The song is *I Whistle a Happy Tune*.

All the elements we need for an "as if" scenario are contained within these lyrics. As I explained earlier, your body doesn't know the difference between actually doing something and intensely *visualizing* doing that very same thing.

Because of that fact, when we visualize ourselves as being confident, as accomplishing the goal we set out to do, we are learning new methods of dealing with our learned and self-imposed fears.

Body language

Whenever I feel afraid
I hold my head erect
And whistle a happy tune
So no one will suspect
I'm afraid.

In the song, the first suggestion is to hold your head erect. Think of a dog that is afraid. Their head is lowered; their eyes are looking up at the object of their fear. They lower their body toward the ground.

- Go to a mirror. Look at yourself in the mirror.
- Balance yourself by putting your feet hip width apart facing front.
- Line up your ears over your shoulders.
- Line up your shoulders over your hipbones.
- Align your hipbones over your ankles.

- Now raise your shoulders to your ears without the help of your arms.
- Roll your shoulders back and squeeze, squeeze, squeeze.
- Breathe normally, count to 10, and relax your knees.
- Now, drop your shoulders.

Isn't that an amazing release? That uncomfortable, achy place between your shoulder blades is your rhomboid muscles. Most times during the day when we're sitting, especially in front of a computer or a keyboard, our chins jut out. This keeps our heads in a misaligned position. When our chins stick out, our shoulders round forward. By doing the simple exercise above, you are straightening your body and releasing a great deal of tension in your sternum (that marvelous chest bone that holds your ribs in place).

Put your head on your shoulders
Doesn't that sound silly? Just as our heads jut out toward the computer, we do the same thing with an audience. We act as though we're trying to sell something. Stop selling. Be velvet and absorb the light.

Pretend you're Elvis and you are wearing a very high collar. Put your index finger on your chin and move your head back toward the high collar. You should feel a stretch in the muscles of your back and neck. If you have been walking around with your head (almost the weight of a bowling ball) jutting way out, you have created neck, shoulder and back tension.

If you look at yourself in the mirror after this exercise, you will see a more aligned, bright and confident you. Isn't it amazing what a few degrees of aligned posture will do?

Get yourself to an <u>Alexander class</u>. It will make a huge difference not only in your performance and in a release of tension, but also in how you present yourself. Explore the <u>Feldenkrais method.</u> Astounding emotional and physical breakthroughs can happen.

What is your body saying?

> *While shivering in my shoes*
> *I strike a careless pose*
> *And whistle a happy tune,*
> *And no one ever knows*
> *I'm afraid.*

What your body is unconsciously saying is an invaluable tool for an actor. But first, you must become conscious of your body language. A fine actor is a master of body language. I am only touching on this subject. It would take volumes to go into this in detail. That's part of your job as an actor.

Joe Navarro, an ex-FBI agent specializing in nonverbal communication, wrote a book that is a gem: *What Every BODY is Saying*. Every performer needs this book in their personal library. It's a great tool.

You can use your thoughts to try to disguise your true emotions all you want, but the limbic system will self-regulate and give off clues. Observing these alarm reactions knowing that they are honest and significant is extremely important; it can even save lives.[1]

An appearance of overconfidence in an audition can be as negative as showing your nerves. For example, a young man walks into an audition and hooks his thumbs inside his waistband on either side of the zipper of his pants This gesture is known as genital framing. You're probably shaking your head and saying, I would never do that. In the same way that we are unconscious about mannerisms that happen on stage, we need to be become more aware of mannerisms that happen in daily life. What you are saying to the auditioners is: I'm a very sexy male. If you're auditioning for the role of *Don Juan*, and you use that gesture deliberately, that's different.

If, in an attempt to do something with your hands, you stick your thumbs in your pocket to make yourself feel more comfortable, you are actually being self-defeating. Did you know that gesture indicates low confidence and low status? You're giving the wrong impression. Instead, when your thumb is sticking out of your pocket, it can often indicate high confidence.

Do you fiddle with your hair continuously? That betrays nerves and uncertainty. It can also look like a nervous tic. Your hair needs to reveal and compliment your face, not hide it.

How do you shake hands? Depending on what country you're in, it will make a big difference. When you greet a panel of auditioners or when you come out to talk to your public in various countries in the world, you should research what is appropriate. An excellent reference is: *Kiss, Bow or Shake Hands (The Best Selling Guide to Doing Business in 60 Countries)*, by Morrison & Conaway.

When you stand on stage waiting for auditioners to choose your next selection, do you cross your hands over your chest protectively? You're cutting yourself off by adopting a defensive stance. Suppose you interlace your fingers or wring your hands? Such behavior is associated with nervousness and sometimes, even with deception. It's not the most positive thing to do. It's important to learn what your body is saying. The minute you finish this book, get Joe's.

Even when you try to cover up what you're feeling, the limbic brain adjusts. You will still betray your real feelings. That simple fact lets us know the adjustment needs to be much deeper than the physical. You need to change your mental attitude not just your gestures and posture.

Positive self-deception

The result of this deception
Is very strange to tell,
For when I fool the people I fear
I fool myself as well!

Isn't this wonderfully obvious? I have experienced this so many times and I teach it in my seminars and in my classes. When I'm feeling down my body reflects it. Isn't that interesting? Even the action of lowering your head, looking down, dampens your mood. Think about that. If I listen to joyous music or I see a good friend unexpectedly round a corner, my heart lifts. Get the direction here? My mood changes. We are in charge of how we choose to approach a situation that makes us uncomfortable. Yes, your limbic brain is still going to give clues of your discomfort, but that's part of being human.

Think of how often we react unconsciously to the non-verbal clues we're getting from others. Think of looking out at the audition panel. How do you feel when they're gazing up at the ceiling, scratching their heads or doodling on a piece of paper? Right, they're not paying attention. If they're not paying attention, how can they judge you? That's not your problem and it's not in your control. Your job is to do your best, harness the tools you have and make them work for you.

Acting "as if" has another perk. Posture that is more confident allows air to fall easily into your lungs. A genuine smile on your face, one that shows in your eyes, is magnetic. Move your shoulders back and show the underside of your arms. Opening your hands and arms shows "I'm here, I'm pliant, I'm ready to give." There are so many postures that command attention or say "look at me," but in a positive way. Our energy affects others.

Don't forget to breathe

I whistle a happy tune,
And every single time
The happiness in the tune.
Convinces me that I'm
Not afraid!

What happens when you whistle? You have to breathe. You have to breathe more deeply. What happens when you breathe more deeply? You oxygenate yourself. You therefore feel better. Oxygen lifts negative emotions and activates the core of your body. Remember what I said about strengthening your core?

That core is your essential command center. It's the physical storehouse of your strength. When you breathe more deeply, your voice is more beautiful. Your playing is better and your performance is going to be better. Certainly your dance, your interpretation or any of the art forms in which you participate, is going to be strengthened by the fact that you are breathing more deeply.

One of the most important things to remember is that the minute we become afraid, our breath becomes shallow. We get away from diaphragmatic breathing which is healthy breathing.

Make-believe

> *Make-believe you're brave*
> *And the trick will take you far;*
> *You may be as brave*
> *As you make believe you are.*
> *You may be as brave*
> *As you as you make believe you are.*

Go back again to the feeling of joy when as children we made believe we were a Princess, or a Pirate King, or a Doctor, a Teacher, an Actor. When we made believe, we were so immersed in the role we had chosen. The fear of what someone else thought of how well we were fulfilling our role-play was immaterial. That is a key for any actor. Yes, every performer is an actor. If you are a dancer, a singer, a guitar player, a trumpet player, you are creating a spell. You are sharing a moment of reality with your audience, a moment of your sensibility.

Remember, the definition of acting is *acting real in an unreal situation*. No matter what avenue of performance, some emotion, some pain, joy, or love will inform and color your playing. It's not just the technique that will move your audience. A good technician is only that, a good technician.

The key to acting "as if" and the place to practice it are in your Zen studio. Here you can take that make-believe world and make it real. You can create a gift for the people in the dark and for your own heart as well.

Personal experience
I can say of myself that when I was in the sheltering arms of stage light and on those boards, I felt protected. It was far easier to make-believe or act out a moment of reality in an unreal situation. So many times in my life, I literally hummed or whistled this song from *The King and I*.

One time, I got thrown out of a dressing room by one of my colleagues. She made me turn around three times and spit on the floor. Why? Because I was whistling in the dressing room and my colleague was quite sure I had brought devastation on our show. The show was fine.

Wrap up
Simply reading this book won't make its methods become reality: not even it you put it under your pillow. Experiment with what works for you and change will occur. No matter how hard you work, don't lose the love and joy that brought you to performance in the first place. Passion is the magic ingredient that transforms you and your audience.

Enjoy this extraordinary three year old boy named Jonathan, who literally falls over with excitement while conducting the 4th Movement of Beethoven's Symphony No. 5.

If you can contact this love, this excitement, this *unashamed enthusiasm*, you have what it takes to achieve your dreams, musical or otherwise. Learn the lessons, the skill, the technique, but keep the joy! You may play under Maestro Jonathan's baton someday and he would be very disappointed if you weren't happy - so would I.

Unfold your myth. ♪

Chapter 11: Summary

Your body does not know the difference between actually doing something and intensely visualizing doing that very same thing.

When we visualize ourselves as being confident, as accomplishing the goal we set out to do, **we are learning new methods of dealing with our learned and self-imposed fears.**

Body Language: Have a friend of yours follow you around for a day and take a few pictures. Pay attention to how you hold your body. How do you stand when you're in a group? How do you hold your shoulders and your head? **What is your body saying about you?**

Straighten up: Get yourself in a neutral position. Without using your arms, raise your shoulders to your ears. Roll them back and squeeze the space between your shoulder blades. Breathe normally. Count to 10, and relax your knees. Now drop your shoulders. Isn't that an amazing release?

Put your head on your shoulders: Stop selling. Be velvet! Absorb the light. Put your index finger on your chin and move your head back toward an imaginary high collar. Feel the stretch of the muscles of your back and neck?

Become very conscious of your body language. A **fine performer is a master of body language**.

Even when you try to cover up what you're feeling, your limbic brain will still betray your true feelings. **The adjustments you need to make are from the inside out. It's all about learning a new mental attitude.**

Don't forget to breathe. It gives us mental clarity, releases tension, and activates our core. The *Cycle of Nine* is a huge help.

Core strength. All the pelvic and trunk muscles are **essential to powerful performance.**

Our energy affects others.

Go back to the feeling of joy when as children we played make-believe. **We were completely immersed in the role we had chosen. The fear of what someone else thought of our role play was immaterial.** Don't lose the joy or the fun!

Chapter 11: Exercises

I told you I would ask again, why do you perform? Now that you have enlarged your viewpoint and have a method to your (artistic) madness, I ask the question again. Remember the answer must not be like the first or the second time. Dig deeper.

Why do you perform?

Body Language

Have a friend take a couple of candid (not posed) photos of you when you are just hanging around, talking with friends or eating.

- What does your posture say about you?

- How do you feel about yourself as you look at these pictures?

- What does your body language express?

Have that same friend, or another, take a couple of pictures with you standing with your shoulders back and your head up. Consciously use positive, confident (not fake) body language.

- What differences do you notice?

- How do the differences make you feel about yourself?

- If you didn't know this person, what would be your first impression?

Your New Script, one more time

Your New Script Summary Make it concise and specific.

Your vision board

What do you see for yourself? **Start writing a list as fast as you can.** Give yourself 10 minutes on a timer. Use ALL of your senses. What do you **see** for yourself? What do you **feel**? What can you **hear**?

Enjoy this process. There won't be a quiz. This is your life. Design it with all your heart and all your passion but remember to dance lightly. On the next two pages, cut out images that reflect what you have listed here. Be flexible, make huge mistakes, grow and be joyous.

Carpe diem. Seize *your* day! **Make your list now:**

What is in focus for your life?

NOTES

Chapter 2
1. Emmons, Shirley and Alma Thomas, *Power Performance for Singers: Transcending the Barriers* (New York Oxford University press 1998) 60.

Chapter 3
1. Oscar Wilde, *The Picture of Dorian Gray* (New York: Signet Classics, The New American Library, 1962), 96.

Chapter 4
1. Dr. Charles Yesalis, (Professor Emeritus, Pennsylvania State University), in discussion with the author, May 2011
2. Blair Tindall, Better Playing Through Chemistry, *New York Times*, October 17, 2004,
3. *Journal of Allergy and Clinical Immunology*, Vol. 84, No. 1, July 1989: 129-30

Chapter 5
1. Benjamin Zander and Rosamund Zander, *The Art of Possibility* (New York: Penguin Group, 2000), 79
2. Ibid. 62

Chapter 7
1. Michael Colgrass, *My Lessons with Kumi* (Utah: Real People Press,2000) 12-13
2. Ibid. 13

Chapter 9
1. Michael Colgrass, *Music Magazine*, November/December 1981.
2. Ibid.

Chapter 10
1. Kofi Busia, editor 2005, 2010, www.kofibusia.com/iyengarbiography/iyengarbio12.php

Chapter 11
1. I Whistle a Happy Tune, *The King & I (lyrics used with permission of Williamson Music)*
2. Joe Navarro, *What Every BODY is Saying*, ed. Marvin Karlins (New York: Harper Collins, 2008)

BIBILOGRAPHY

Busia, Kofi. *Iyengar Biography* 2000, 2010, www.kofibusia.com/iyengarbiography/

Canfield, Jack, Mark Victor Hansen, Les Hewitt. *The Power of Focus: How to Hit Your Business, Personal and Financial Targets with Absolute Certainty* Florida, Health Communications, Inc. 2000.

Colgrass, Michael. *My Lessons with Kumi* Utah, Real People Press 2000.

Eamon's, Shirley and Alma Thomas. *Power Performance for Singers: Transcending the him Barriers,* New York, Oxford University Press 1998.

Journal of Allergy and Clinical Immunology, Vol. 84, No. 1, July 1989.

MacLaine, Shirley. *I'm Over All That* New York: Atria Books, 2011.

Maslow, Abraham. *Toward a Psychology of Being,* 2nd Ed New York: Van Nostrand, 1968.

Navarro, Joe. *What Every BODY is Saying,* ed. Marvin Karlins New York: Harper Collins, 2008.

Wilde, Oscar. *The Picture of Dorian Gray* New York: Signet Classics, The New American Library, 1962.

Zander, Rosamund and Benjamin Zander. *The Art of Possibility* New York: Penguin Group, 2000.

Acknowledgements

First, I must thank my beloved students who inspired this book with their questions and their ongoing artistic quest. Their bright spirits brought back to life the love of my craft and my art. I thought that had all gone up in the flame of burnout long ago. Thank you to Dr. Donna Connolly, my stubborn friend who dragged me kicking and screaming to NJCU and somehow divined I was a teacher.

Lina Maddaford fueled my artistry more than anyone did. She called me her Callas and I treasured her love and respect. Josef, your predictions came true. Irene darling, you took my breath away when I was 12 years old – you still do. Andrew Farkas, you taught me so much. You and Peter Bence know far more about opera than most opera singers. Thank you.

Maestra Sara Sforni-Corti in Milano, what you taught me about voice would fill an entire book. You opened my eyes and I hope I do the same for my students. Singing must never hurt. It is as natural as good breathing. Armen Boyajian, my, we had adventures. You taught me in a relatively short time a world about form and style. I couldn't have done *Amneris*, *Santuzza* or *Regina* without you!

Ralph Bassett, I wouldn't still be on this planet if it were not for you. Do you still think you're not my guardian angel? Don't those wings give you problems when you sit down?

Michael Hirsch, my director and inspired reader who clarified and illuminated so much. To my first draft editor, Steven Derek Brown, thank you. A heartfelt thank you to David Mayfield, my clear-eyed colleague. My Editor in Chief, Freddie my sister, my friend, heartfelt thanks for each word and each time you gently said, "Read it out loud again."

George Heymont, we've talked from the Egyptian pyramids to San Francisco, from the world of opera to the Huffington Post over a stack of years. You even made me a cover girl. You are a treasure. Your invaluable commentary helped me immeasurably. Your writing and knowledge is a constant source of inspiration. Thank you.

Lee A. Olsen, my beloved mentor, I can never repay the support you gave me from the moment we shook hands onstage at the Rosarian Academy in Palm Beach when I had just won First Prize. Without you, I would never have escaped my cage and flown around the world to sing. I never knew what fun was until you taught me. I miss you.

Charles Kingsford your generosity allowed me to keep going when I would have had to give up. Your music will continue through my students.

Jorge, my patient, loving partner; thank you for your capacity to encourage and accept all I am. Great soul, I love you.

Author's Bio

Adria Firestone has been on the world's stages in straight theater, opera, concerts and musical theater for most of her life. From *Carmen* to *Family Guy*, from Shanghai to the Pacific Rim, from Cairo to Canada, from Desiree in *A Little Night Music*, to her award-winning Aldonza in *The Man of La Mancha*, Adria Firestone has experienced just about every facet of performance.

Adria found her voice and absorbed the culture and the language when she lived in Italy. She thrived on eight shows a week and was nominated for another Carbonell for Jenny in *Threepenny Opera*.

For the past 20 years, Adria has given seminars, workshops and master classes in performance techniques, self-help, presentation skills, and controlling stage fright. Adria is a life and career coach with international clientele. She has been teaching at New Jersey City University for over eight years. She teaches Voice, Acting for Singers, Movement for Actors and Speech for Performance.

Her private clients work with Adria on career planning and transition, controlling stage fright, voice and role interpretation.

To learn more, visit:

www.harnessyourzebra.com
www.changingmyself.tv
www.adriafirestone.com

www.ingramcontent.com/pod-product-compliance
Lightning Source LLC
Chambersburg PA
CBHW080734300426
44114CB00019B/2584